The Shocking Hi

Zina Cohen

Contains Biographies of the 40 Founding Fathers of the European Union

Dedicated to Tina, my seven-year-old daughter: this book has been written in the interests of your future.

Contents List

Foreword

It isn't enough for Britain to get out of the European Union. We must destroy it before the organisation does any more damage to the nations and people of Europe. Once again it is up to Britain to defeat Germany. Hopefully, this will be for the last time.

Destroying the EU will also protect us from treacherous Remainers who will, without a doubt, make every effort imaginable to lie and cheat and attempt to get us back into the most fascist organisation ever created.

The European Union is all about power and money. Freedom, democracy, dignity, tradition, respect and culture were never ever part of the EU philosophy.

The EU, which was designed and built by Nazis to turn Hitler's dreams into reality, needs to be destroyed and that means exposing the roots to the light.

This book shines a searchlight on the European Union and exposes its dark beginnings with ruthless accuracy. She explains how and why the Nazis built the EU.

She explains what Tony Blair and the BBC won't tell you (and what Gary Lineker possibly doesn't know) about the History of the EU.

Jack King (author of, Indisputable Evidence Proving the EU was Created by Nazis)

Introduction

I doubt if 1 in 1,000 of the EU's supporters understands why and how the European Union was created – or why it exists at all. I very much doubt if any of the many politicians and celebrities who have spoken out against Britain leaving the EU have bothered to investigate the history of the European Union. If they had they would probably be less enthusiastic about allying themselves to an organisation which is probably the most fascist organisation ever created – and one which was designed and built by enthusiastic Nazis.

Most of our politicians are disreputable, dishonest, unreliable, arrogant, greedy and quite stupid. But those who are committed Remainers, and who have shown themselves enemies of democracy, and eager to overthrow the will of the people, have taken all these traits to new heights.

The people who run the European Union these days have been very successful in covering up the organisation's history. Efficient propagandists in the style of Goebbels have brilliantly suppressed the organisation's past and have whitewashed the personal histories of its founders. They have efficiently created a superficially credible history and raison d'etre to replace the EU's real history and its real purpose. By spending billions of taxpayers' money on propaganda (disguised as 'education') they have not only hidden the EU's Nazi secrets but they have also succeeded in isolating and demonising those who dare to tell the truth. The EU has been so successful in misdirecting the public that anyone who dares to tell the truth about the EU's background is likely to be dismissed as a conspiracy theorist.

The EU has been very bad for Britain in a number of ways (there is a summary at the back of this book) but very few people realise that the EU was never intended to make our lives better.

The EU was created to promote and protect big German businesses and all the truly bad things about the EU (the absence of democracy, the endless rules, the diminishing freedom) were written into the EU from the beginning. Right from the start, the European

Union has been an organisation which has not regarded democracy very highly; has, indeed, regarded it as a nuisance.

The Nazis, and the various officers of the early European Union, all regarded democracy as an uncomfortable and unnecessary part of government. It cannot, therefore, be surprising that this feeling is the basic principle upon which the modern EU is built.

A common complaint today is that the European Union is undemocratic but this should not be a surprise to anyone for the EU's institutions were never designed to have any sense of democracy about them. The EU which exists today was planned in precise detail by Ribbentrop, Funk and other Nazis who regarded democracy as an uncomfortable luxury which could not be afforded.

Today, the vast majority of the EU's many supporters are uninformed about the purpose of the EU. They haven't bothered to study the organisation's history; instead, they have accepted the sanitised version of the EU's history and they haven't made the effort to look behind the screen to see when and why, and with what very specific purpose, the EU was created.

The basic role of Government is to use our taxes to make our lives safer and to protect our country from danger so that citizens can go about their business safely and without fear. If the Government can make our lives a little better that is a bonus. The idea is that the Government should spot risks, assess their importance and deal with them. But politicians have long since forgotten all their primary, traditional responsibilities. And many MPs seem to have forgotten that they were elected to Parliament to represent the local electors. Nearly three quarters of all MPs are overt Remainers – even though many of them come from constituencies which voted to leave. In other words, the MPs concerned are acting in a way which is contrary to the majority of their constituents.

Moreover, they are deliberately aiding and abetting the enemy (in this case a bunch of eurocrats) who are intent on controlling our lives. That used to be called treason.

The EU is promoted as a democratic and liberal organisation which puts people first. It doesn't take much of an examination to see that the European Union fails in all of these criteria. It is decidedly undemocratic and illiberal and the only people it puts first are the bureaucrats who run the various branches of the organisation.

There is, it is true, a European parliament but this can only advise and has no power. It is used merely to rubber stamp the decisions of the European Commissioners and their underlings. Members of the European Parliament (MEPs) are as self-serving as other EU employees. In addition to huge salaries, they receive absurdly generous expense accounts with cash being reimbursed without there being any need to show that it has been spent.

Almost all the laws the EU produces (they like to call them 'regulations' but it seems more appropriate to describe as a law anything which carries on its back a State backed punishment) are designed to stifle entrepreneurs and to crush small businesses. This is no accident; it is deliberate policy. When the Nazis and IG Farben created the European Union the aim was to ensure the success and profitability of large German industries. It is no exaggeration to say that the aim was to take over the commercial world. (I wonder how many enthusiasts who wave EU flags realise that the EU was created by the very same people who built Auschwitz.)

The EU is all about control as opposed to freedom. There is absolutely no acknowledgement of any democratic process and there is no consideration for culture, dignity, respect, history or community. Unelected bureaucrats create new laws without any thought for the consequences. So, for example, eurocrats promoted diesel cars without properly investigating the consequences and then, when it appeared that diesel cars were more likely to pollute the environment than petrol driven cars, they simply changed their minds – wrecking the car industry and leaving millions of people facing capital losses and additional tax burdens merely because they had followed the EU's advice.

The one surprising thing, perhaps, is the fact that the campaign to leave the EU seems to have shown us just how ignorant the various parts of the establishment can be.

It sometimes seems that the entire British establishment has united in support of the Nazi inspired European Union. The Remainers include: Parliament, the Speaker of the House of Commons, just about all large international companies, the banks (British and foreign), the Bank of England, the Archbishop of Canterbury and much of the Church of England, the civil service, the professions, most of the media and a motley collection of celebrities.

4

The Government of Theresa May has been duty bound to make an attempt to pursue Brexit but the whole thing has been done with great reluctance. They have been supported by former President Obama of the United States of America and the Prime Minister of Japan. (The support for the Remainers' cause from Obama, a hypocritical blah blah specialist, was an influential factor in ensuring that the Remainers lost the vote.)

The Remainers have taken every opportunity to trash our culture and our history and to trash the loyal British who have dared to defend their nation in public.

I wonder how many of those who have fought so hard against their nation's interests, and for the interests of the European Union, realise that they have been fighting for an organisation which was designed by Nazis for the furtherance of the Nazi dream. I wonder how many enthusiastic celebrities (some of them Jewish) realise that the very same people who built the Auschwitz concentration camp, and made the gas used to kill several million Jews, also built the European Union.

The fact is that, whether they know it or not, the British Establishment is now dominated by neo Nazis. The evidence proves, without any room for doubt, that all British Remainers, whether they are politicians, celebrities or bankers, are traitors.

Foreigners such as Obama (the only man to receive the Nobel Prize for Peace without actually doing anything for Peace) who try to interfere with the democratic process should know that they too are seen as fascists and Neo Nazis.

This book does not deal with the corruption, dishonesty and incompetence now prevalent within the European Union. Nor does it deal with the damage done to our culture and our way of life. These issues are dealt with in depth by other authors such as Vernon Coleman in his book *OFPIS: The Truth about the EU*.

In this book I have concentrated on the history of the European Union – how and why it was created and why it exists today. No one who reads this book can possibly remain enthusiastic about the European Union unless they are a committed Nazi or a lover of the Deutschland Uber Allies philosophy. It is impossible that any rational person could want their country to retain membership of an organisation with such an evil background and such an evil purpose.

My fear is that the material in this book will be dismissed by the European Union propaganda machine. The EU has always been very good at protecting itself from the truth.

Commentators who have drawn attention to the fact that the EU is identical to the federal Europe planned by Funk et al have always been dismissed as paranoid conspiracy theorists. The fact that the terms 'European Economic Community' and 'European Union' were first used by the Nazis has been dismissed as nothing more than a coincidence.

Hopefully, this attempt to air the truth about the European Union will be more successful.

Chapter 1

The Bank for International Settlements

For decades, the world has been wrecked by three utterly corrupt and self-serving organisations: the International Monetary Fund, the World Bank and the Bank for International Settlements.

Of these three, the only one which concerns us directly is the third: the Bank for International Settlements, known as the BIS. And to understand how the Nazis succeeded in creating the EU it is first necessary to study the BIS.

To discover the truth it is, as always, simply necessary to follow the money.

The trail connecting IG Farben, a bunch of ambitious Nazi crooks, some unscrupulous self-serving Americans, the Bank for International Settlements (the BIS), the Bundesbank and the European Central Bank is not difficult to follow.

For decades, the Bank for International Settlements, then and now the most powerful bank in the world, has been so secretive that it is not even mentioned in most books about the Second World War. Today, it is still the central bank for the world's central banks but it is no exaggeration to say that without the BIS and IG Farben there would have been no Second World War. And there would be no European Union.

The activities of the BIS were reported in the official diaries of Henry Morgenthau, the US Treasury Secretary at the time. Those diaries, and other documents, showed just how important a part the bank played in the Second World War.

The BIS was created in 1930 by the world's central banks, including the Federal Reserve Bank in New York and the Bank of England in London. The BIS was, however, the brainchild of Hjalmar Horace Greeley Schacht, the president of the German Reichsbank and the Nazi Minister of Economics. Schacht, who had grown up in Brooklyn, was assisted by Emil Puhl. During the War,

Schacht was replaced by Walther Funk, Hitler's economics adviser. Emil Puhl retained important positions at both institutions and was the link between the BIS and the Nazis.

Schact had deliberately set up the BIS because he knew that there was eventually going to be a war between Germany and other European countries. The idea was that the BIS would enable the Nazis to maintain channels of communication between Berlin and financial institutions around the world. Schacht made sure that the BIS's charter emphasised that the Bank would remain immune from censure or closure during war.

Moreover, Schacht was clever enough to disguise the BIS's main purpose by claiming that the BIS would help Germany provide the Allies with financial reparations owed after World War I.

However, instead of money flowing from Germany to the Allies, it went in the other direction and was used to help Hitler build up a war chest for the coming conflict.

The Nazis were undoubtedly helped in this by the fact that the first presidents of the BIS, who were American, were easy to deal with. (One of the first presidents of the BIS was an American called Leon Fraser who had been a tabloid journalist and who had little or no background in banking.) The BIS, the central bank for central bankers, quickly became the most important and powerful bank in the world.

In March 1938, Hitler's armies moved into Austria and one of the first things the troops did was to steal the nation's gold and transport it to vaults controlled by the BIS.

More Nazi troops tried to do the same thing when they marched into Prague. Nazi soldiers demanded that the directors of the Czech National Bank hand over Czechoslovakia's supply of gold – $48 million worth. The directors replied that they had already moved the gold to the BIS with instructions that it be sent to the Bank of England. Unfazed by this, the Nazis simply instructed the Czechs to tell the Bank of England to send the gold back to Switzerland.

In fact, the Governor of the Bank of England (a flamboyant and traitorous exhibitionist called Montagu Norman) made life easier for the Nazis by immediately authorising the BIS in Switzerland to take $48 million worth of gold from the Bank of England's account and to put it straight into the German account so that it was immediately available for the Nazis to use. By 1939, when the War began, the BIS had made many millions available to the Nazis.

In 1940 an American, Thomas McKittrick, was appointed president of BIS as a replacement for Leon Fraser. McKittrick was a lawyer and a friend of the Nazi party and he turned BIS into an arm of the Reichsbank. Fluent in German, McKittrick had previously worked for Lee, Higginson and Company and had made large loans to the Nazis. There is no doubt that McKittrick's sympathies were with Germany. Indeed, in 1940, during the War, he went to Berlin and had a meeting at the Reichsbank with the Gestapo.

And the BIS under McKittrick continued to act as a middleman for stolen gold.

By the start of World War II, the BIS was already controlled by Hitler. McKittrick was the president of the Bank but the other directors included Hitler's economics adviser, Dr Walther Funk, Emil Puhl, a director of the Reichsbank, Hermann Schmitz, the head of the Nazi conglomerate known as IG Farben (the company which built the concentration camps and supplied the poison gas for the gas chambers) and Baron Kurt von Schroder, a banker and Gestapo officer.

Throughout the War, the BIS accepted and stored looted gold and carried out foreign exchange deals on behalf of Hitler. Much of the gold accepted by the BIS came from the teeth and belongings of concentration camp victims. Hitler's economics adviser, Walther Funk, worked with Heinrich Himmler (a leading Nazi and head of the SS) to ensure that gold from concentration camp victims was put into a special Reichsbank account. Gold from jewels, spectacle frames, watches, cigarette cases and teeth was melted down into 20 kilogram bars and sent to Switzerland where it could be 'laundered' through the Swiss National Bank before being made available to the Nazis, via the BIS, as 'clean' gold. McKittrick, who constantly provided the Reichsbank with intelligence material, helped the Nazis take control of occupied countries and their banks.

Astonishingly, the Bank of England continued to cooperate with the BIS throughout the War, although the British directors Sir Otto Niemeyer and Montagu Norman must have known that the BIS was effectively Hitler's inexhaustible piggy bank. Without the BIS's cooperation, the Nazis would have run out of money for arms and the Second World War would have probably never started or would have ended within a year or so at most.

In June 1940, $228 million worth of gold which the Belgian Government was trying to send to safety was intercepted by the BIS and redirected to the Reichsbank.

Money stolen from Holland also went via the BIS to the Nazis.

Amazingly, the Bank of England, as one of the founders of the BIS, continued to have a strong relationship with the bank and to receive dividends from it. (It was not until the end of the War that it became clear that most of the money paid out in dividends had gone to Germany.)

In February 1942, two months after Pearl Harbour, the Reichsbank and the German and Italian Governments decided that McKittrick should remain President of the BIS for the duration of the War. In one Nazi document it was stated that 'McKittrick's opinions are safely known to us'. The faith of the Nazis was well placed, for the BIS continued to provide gold for their use.

Throughout the Second World War, McKittrick travelled around Europe quite freely, on occasion being escorted by Himmler's special SS police force. According to the author Charles Higham, McKittrick even went back to America for a meeting with the Federal Reserve Bank and then returned to Berlin where he reported to the Reichsbank.

Not everyone ignored what was happening in Switzerland.

In his book *The Hidden Enemy*, published in 1943, Heinz Pol wrote: 'The Bank for International Settlements in neutral Basel, Switzerland, has been, since 1941, almost entirely controlled by Axis representatives…'

In 1943, Congressman Jerry Voorhis of California called for an investigation into the BIS, demanding to know why an American was the President of a bank which was being used by and for the Nazis.

Nothing happened.

Again, in early 1944, Congressman John F Coffee asked similar questions. He pointed out that the majority of the board of the BIS was made up of Nazi officials but that American money was being deposited in the bank.

At an International Monetary Conference held at Bretton Woods in 1944, a Norwegian economist called William Keilhau called for the BIS to be dissolved and for there to be an investigation of the bank's books and records. In Britain, Lord Keynes and Sir Anthony Eden decided that the BIS should be allowed to remain active until after the end of the War. Keynes said that the BIS should be allowed to continue until a new world bank and an international monetary fund could be set up. Amazingly, the argument for retaining the BIS was that the bank would help restore and rebuild Germany at the end of the War. It was argued that if the BIS were dissolved, the Germans would fear that their relationship with America might not survive the end of the War.

Nevertheless, despite high level support, it was decided by the Americans that the BIS should be liquidated.

Astonishingly, however, McKittrick simply refused to accept the decision. He wrote to America and to Britain arguing that when the War ended the Allies would have to pay huge sums of money to Germany and that these would be best paid through the BIS. He did not explain why he felt that the Allies would have to pay huge sums to Germany but he did also argue that the BIS would be essential to help provide loans for the rebuilding of Germany after the War.

When questioned about the gold which the Nazis had stolen, McKittrick replied, apparently with a straight face, that it was being held in the vaults of the Reichsbank so that it could be returned to its owners after the end of the War.

In May of 1944, it was McKittrick and his staff who dealt with the $378 million in gold which the Nazi Government sent to Switzerland for use after the War.

By then the Nazis realised that they were losing the War and the gold (some of which had been stolen from the national banks of Austria, Belgium, Czechoslovakia and Holland and some of which had been melted down from gold collected from jewellery, spectacle frames and teeth of murdered prisoners in the concentration camps) was intended to be used by the Nazis after the end of the War. McKittrick must have known this but he and the BIS were happy to deal with the stolen gold.

In 1948, the BIS was ordered to hand the looted gold over to the Allies.

The amount handed over came to just $4 million.

No one at the BIS ever admitted what had happened to the hundreds of millions in stolen gold which had been deposited there by the Nazis. No one ever found the $374 million which was missing from the money sent for the use of the Nazis after the end of the War.

There was ample evidence to show that McKitrick had willingly cooperated with the Nazis but after the War he was given important posts in America including being made vice-president of the Chase National Bank. (This was perhaps not surprising since during the War the Chase Bank in Paris had helped finance the Nazis and had refused to release funds belonging to Jews.)

After the end of the War, Karl Blessing, a Nazi who had controlled an army of slave labourers in Germany's concentration camps, returned to the BIS and became president of the Bundesbank.

Nevertheless, it was felt that someone from the BIS needed to be punished and so in 1945, Emil Puhl, who had been vice president of the Reichsbank and a director of the BIS, was one of the few civilian Nazis to be found guilty of war crimes. Puhl had been responsible for moving Nazi gold during the War – knowing that much of the gold had come from prisoners in Germany's various concentration camps. Puhl was sentenced to a modest five years in prison but he appears to have served very little of this and in 1950 he was invited by his friend Thomas McKittrick to visit America as his guest. Puhl, a Nazi economist, director of the BIS and the Reichsbank had been McKittrick's go between with the Nazis.

Despite the decision made by the Americans and the British, the Bank for International Settlements was not dissolved after the end of the War.

Instead, it went from strength to strength.

In 1954, the European Coal and Steel Community (the forerunner of the European Union) asked the United States for a loan of $100 million. Inevitably, the loan was arranged with the help of the BIS – the bank which had worked closely with the Nazis during World War II.

Legally untouchable and existing outside all jurisdictions, the BIS was created to act as the central bank for central bankers. It is disturbing to realise that the BIS is still the most powerful financial institution in the world though many politicians, economists and bankers have never even heard of it.

Current directors of the BIS include Mark Carney, the Canadian born governor of the Bank of England and enthusiastic supporter of the EU.

It should be no surprise that Carney has repeatedly warned of the hazards associated with Britain leaving the EU.

Chapter 2

Traitors at the Bank of England

The modern Bank of England has repeatedly warned about the consequences of leaving the European Union. Carney has consistently claimed that terrible things will happen if the UK dares to go through with leaving the EU.

Indeed, the Bank's enthusiastic support of the EU and its repeated, often hysterical criticisms of Brexit , have surprised many who previously understood the Bank of England was expected to stay out of internal or international politics.

However, no one should really have been surprised.

History shows that the Bank of England has often worked against the interests of the British people.

In the period before the Second World War, Sir Montagu Norman, the director of the Bank of England was a strong supporter of Hjalmar Schacht, the German Central Bank President who was a strong supporter of Hitler and the Nazi party. Norman, who was godfather to one of Schacht's grandchildren, was also a founder and director of the Bank for International Settlements.

It has been established that during the War, Sir Montagu Norman helped the Nazis steal Czech gold from the Bank for International Settlements.

When he resigned from the Bank of England in 1944, Norman, who should have been tried as a traitor, was raised to the peerage as Baron Norman of St Clere in the County of Kent. He may well have been the leading Nazi supporter in the House of Lords.

Norman was not the first public servant to betray the people who paid his salary – and he probably won't be the last.

Today, the Bank of England is still an enthusiastic supporter of the European Union.

The current holder of the post of Governor of the Bank of England is a Canadian called Mark Carney who is a former employee of Goldman Sachs, the investment bank which is renowned as 'the vampire squid on the face of humanity' and which is believed by many to be the most evil and irresponsible bank in the world.

And, inevitably perhaps, as I have already pointed out, Carney is also a Director of the Bank for International Settlements – the bank which helped Hitler rise to power.

Chapter 3

Germany before World War II: The Role of IG Farben

There have, of course, been dreams of a united Europe for centuries. Charlemagne and Napoleon both wanted to conquer Europe and to create a single country out of a ragbag of nations. But only the Nazis, with the help of a cartel called IG Farben, succeeded in turning a dream into a reality.

The history of the European Union really begins in the 1920s.

In 1925, a group of important German companies (Agfa, Bayer, BASF, Hoechst and other German companies) formed a cartel called IG Farben. Their aim was to obtain control of global markets in key industrial sectors – specifically: chemicals, pharmaceuticals and petrochemicals. History shows quite clearly that it was the formation of this cartel, and the creation of IG Farben, which led directly to the Second World War (and all its associated atrocities) and the European Union.

Hitler and the Nazi party did not simply dream of uniting Europe: they dreamt of ensuring that Germany would control a unified Europe (which would be called the United States of Europe) in every conceivable way.

It is no coincidence that both Hitler and the EU aimed to control the people through an unelected, autocratic bureaucracy. The Nazis replaced democracy with an oligarchy controlled by bureaucrats and that, of course, is exactly what the European Union has done.

It was in 1933 that IG Farben began to finance the rising German politician called Adolf Hitler, and his National Socialist German Workers' Party (already known as the Nazi party). The directors of IG Farben believed that the Nazis would help them in their goal of controlling markets world-wide. It was one of Hitler's associates,

Walther Funk, (who was later the designer of the European Union and the euro) who persuaded the industrialists to finance the Nazis.

The relationship between IG Farben and the Nazis was symbiotic.

IG Farben gave millions of reichsmarks to the Nazis and in return, the Nazis gave the company control over industries in the countries which the Germans occupied. The aim was to create a massive European Market for IG Farben's products. Later, the Nazis also helped IG Farben by providing cheap labour through its concentration camps. (One of the concentration camps at Auschwitz was built by IG Farben. The company also made the poison gas used to kill inmates.)

Right from the start, Adolf Hitler was keen to develop a federal state of Europe, controlled by Germany.

In 1936, Hitler instructed Joachim von Ribbentrop, who was at the time Ambassador to the United Kingdom, to negotiate an Anglo-German alliance as a preliminary to the development of a United States of Europe. When this failed, Ribbentrop talked to leaders of Italy and Japan and suggested that the three countries join together and divide up the British Empire among themselves.

(Mussolini, the Italian leader, had invented fascism in 1919 and had, in 1933, talked of a need for political unity in Europe. Mussolini and Hitler shared a yearning for a federal state of Europe.)

By 1938, the Nazis were desperate for more funds. Equipping an army and starting a war needed a lot of money.

When Hitler's forces crossed the border into Czechoslovakia, the Nazis arranged for 23.1 metric tons of Czechoslovakian gold, which was held in the Bank for International Settlements (BIS), to be transferred into the Reichsbank account at the BIS. The Nazis were helped in this by Sir Montagu Norman who was governor of the Bank of England. A little later, the BIS helped move another 27 metric tons of Czechoslovak gold into the Nazi's account. (If the sums had been smaller it would have been called 'stealing'.)

The Bank for International Settlements (BIS) had been created in 1930 by the governors of the Reichsbank and the Bank of England. The BIS had been created to act as the central bank for central bankers and it played an essential part in the growth of Nazi Germany. As I have pointed out earlier, it is no exaggeration to say that without the help of the BIS, World War II would have probably not taken place and the European Union would not now exist. Today, the BIS is the most powerful and secretive bank in the world.

During World War II, the BIS helped Hitler a good deal by investing a great deal of money in Germany and by legitimatising the Third Reich's activities. It was the BIS which helped the Reichsbank appropriate Jewish businesses and steal the funds which would finance the Nazi war machine.

In 1939, Hermann Schmitz joined the board of BIS. This was an important move for the Nazis since Schmitz was the CEO of IG Farben.

During the Second World War, IG Farben's directors and managers ran a private concentration camp called IG Auschwitz. The gas capsules used in the notorious gas chambers throughout Germany were made by a subsidiary of IG Farben and sold to the Nazis. The gas used was Zyklon B – a cyanide based pesticide.

(One of the few people to be executed for using the gas was Bruno Tesch, a chemist. Tesch was executed because he knew that the gas being used was sold to kill people. The company's executives, who were in charge of the operation and who benefited from the profits, were largely unpunished. Indeed, a number of men who had become exceedingly rich from the money made by exploiting concentration camp workers were allowed to keep the money they'd made and to play important roles in post War Germany and the developing European Union.)

In that same year, 1939, Walther Funk was appointed a director of the BIS and president of the Reichsbank.

Funk, a former journalist who had joined the Nazi party in 1931, was already Hitler's economics minister and was, as already explained, the man who encouraged IG Farben and other large German companies to fund the Nazi war machine. (According to Heinz Pol, Funk had already earned a small fortune writing propaganda pamphlets for Thyssen – another large German company.)

On January 23, 1939, Walter Hallstein, who was Dean of the Faculty of Law and Economics at the University of Rostock, in Germany, gave a propaganda speech about the restructuring of Europe. The speech was part of the preparation for war by the Nazi regime and their powerful partners the oil and drug cartel IG Farben. The Nazis had already annexed Austria and the Czech territories of

Bohemia and Moravia, and in his speech Hallstein describes the planned German conquest of the rest of Europe and the subjugation of the continent. In due course, Hallstein became an officer in the German army.

In 1938, Hallstein had been part of the official Nazi delegation to Rome. There is no little irony in the fact that some years later, Hallstein (who should have been shot as a war criminal) would return to Rome to sign the Treaty setting up the European Union. Today, Hallstein is revered as the first president of the European Commission.

In a letter dated 20th July 1940, executives from IG Farben (which was by then far the world's largest chemical and pharmaceutical cartel) responded to a request from the Nazi government with a blueprint for a 'new economic order' in Europe.

The letter from IG Farben discussed the need for a common European currency, common European laws and a European court – all to be under the control of the coalition between the Nazis and themselves.

The IG Farben plan was for the new Europe to be under the control of IG Farben and the senior Nazis. France had surrendered a month earlier, and both the Nazi leaders and the IG Farben executives were already thinking of how they could best organise Europe under their control. The plan was that the Nazis would take military and political control and IG Farben would take control of the chemical and pharmaceutical markets throughout Europe. It is no accident that the EU opposes democracy and openness and that secrecy, fraud, theft, waste and corruption have repeatedly (and undeniably) been shown to be integral to the EU's way of doing things. The name of the organisation has changed (it began as a Community, became a Market and is now a Union) as the original aims of the founders have become closer.

Two days later, a meeting was held at the Reich Economic Ministry under the chairmanship of the Minister, Walther Funk. The meeting discussed the reorganisation of the 'continental economy' under German control and the incorporation of occupied territories within the 'Great German economy'. Even the question of a new European currency was discussed.

19

IG Farben's need for cheap labour was so great that the company had built a huge factory at Auchswitz where there was a huge reservoir of slave labour. Bayer, the company's pharmaceutical division tested its drugs on prisoners. IG Farben also made huge amounts of money by providing the gas for the killing of prisoners in concentration camps throughout Germany.

And all the time the Nazis were planning how they would control Europe after the War – whether they won or lost.

The truth about what was happening in Europe was widely available in the 1940s to anyone who was interested.

Heinz Pol, the former editor of a newspaper in Berlin, had fled to America and in 1943 he published a book entitled *The Hidden Enemy: The German Threat to Post-War Peace*. Pol's book is without a doubt one of the most important books about German imperialism and German ambitions and, therefore, the European Union, but it is rarely mentioned and almost unobtainable.

Pol, a German citizen, was born in Berlin where he became assistant editor of *The Vossiche Zeitung*. Arrested by the Nazis in 1933 for political opposition, he escaped to Prague and then to Paris. He later went to America and became a United States citizen. In 1940 he had published a book entitled *Suicide of a Democracy*, about the surrender of France.

In his book, Pol explained that Germany realised that the War was lost and was planning to preserve its domination over Europe by doing deals with the Allies. Pol was perhaps the first person (outside the OSS) to realise that the BIS was playing a vital part in the Nazi plan.

Pol claimed that the BIS was the link between Germany and the Allies and was helping with negotiations which would enable Germany to dominate post War Europe. Pol also argued that post War German leaders would trick the rest of the world into believing that they had abandoned Nazi ideals.

'To obtain a peace, which would leave them in power,' he wrote 'they will suddenly flaunt 'European spirit' and offer worldwide 'cooperation'. They will chatter about liberty, equality and fraternity. They will, all of a sudden, make up to the Jews. They will swear to live up to the demands of the Atlantic Charter and any other charter. They will share power with everybody and they will even let others rule for a while. They will do all this and more, if only they are allowed to keep some positions of power and control, that is, the only positions that count: in the army, were it even reduced to a few thousand men; in the key economic organisations; in the courts; in the universities; in the schools.'

And Pol was absolutely right. He had predicted with startling accuracy just how the Nazis would win the peace. After 1945, Nazis took many of the key positions in the new post War Germany. Former war criminals were quietly forgiven and their sins brushed under the carpet. Men who had organised concentration camps were allowed to keep the fortunes they had made.

The EU has meant that Germany has boomed.

Today, Greece, Italy, Spain and France are all in serious trouble but Germany continues to grow stronger every year.

Heinz Pol's book provides the best view of Hitler's Germany. The author claimed that what he described as 'German super-imperialism' had been conceived at the end of the 19th century and that Hitler's plan to take over Europe was an extension of a threat which had been in existence for over half a century.

In *The Hidden Enemy*, Pol warned that the Nazis were already preparing for their post-War victory – regardless of whether they lost or won the War itself. He suggested that the only way to stop German imperialism was to kill all the leading Nazis. 'Everyone belonging to (the party) is personally responsible for all the murders, plunders and other crimes committed by the Nazi regime. Their physical destruction is absolutely necessary.'

After the War ended, IG Farben's divisions were allowed to keep their profits, although in 1945, at the Nuremberg trials, the US Prosecutor stated that: 'without IG Farben, the Second World War would not have been possible'.

The Prosecutor's claim may sound like an exaggeration but it is undeniable that IG Farben financed and helped plan Hitler's attempts to annexe the rest of Europe and then the rest of the world. This was done for commercial rather than political reasons. IG Farben was eager to achieve control of the global chemical, oil and drug markets and using force seemed the most efficient way to overcome the competition. IG Farben financed the Nazi party and transformed what had once been a democracy into a dictatorship.

Chapter 4

The 40 Founding Fathers of the European Union

The European Union has always had difficulty when trying to describe its own founding fathers. But it has overcome its difficulties by ignoring the individuals whose Nazi background was impossible to hide (airbrushing them out of existence) and in 'sanitising' the backgrounds of those individuals who could not be ignored.

Here are short biographies of the founding fathers of the European Union. Nearly all of them were members of the Nazi party.

The EU's Founding Fathers are listed here in alphabetical order.

Finally, it is important to remember that the Nazis would not have been able to succeed in their ultimate aim (setting up the European Union) without the very real help of the United States – provided by Allen Dulles, John Foster Dulles, Thomas McKittrick and John McCloy. Although these four may not have been official members of the Nazi party, they were enthusiastic supporters of the Nazi party's aims and they worked tirelessly to support the Nazi cause, and its ambitions, during and after the Second World War. All four should have been tried and executed as traitors and war criminals. (They are detailed in this chapter.)

Moreover, there is no doubt that at least two Britons (Oswald Moseley and Montagu Norman) played a vital role in helping the Nazis acquire the power to enable them to create the European Union.

Hermann Abs (German 1901-1994)
Hermann Abs was a bank director who helped Hitler enormously by taking over Jewish banks which were forcibly purchased at low prices. The money was then used to build the Nazi war machine.

During the War, Abs was a member of a secret group formed in 1943 and known as the Committee for Foreign Economic Affairs – a group of bankers and businessmen who met to discuss Germany's future after the end of the War. The group included Ludwig Erhard, Ludger Westrick and Karl Blessing.

After the War a friend of his, Charles Gunston of the Bank of England, asked Abs to help rebuild German banking – though Abs had been arrested as a war criminal and sentenced to death in his absence. Gunston worked for the Bank of England as the manager of the German desk and was a senior official in the British occupational authority after the War. Gunston cared nothing about the atrocities perpetrated by the Nazis. All he wanted to do was to help rebuild the German banks. To this end he recruited Abs who was high on a list of Nazi officials who were to be arrested as war criminals. Gunston protected Abs to help Germany rebuild its banking system ready to continue Hitler's work.

Thanks to help from his friends at the Bank of England, Abs was not executed or even imprisoned, and by 1948, he was deputy head of the Reconstruction Loan Corporation and President of the Bank Deutsche Lander. Unbelievably, it was then Abs who decided which German companies should receive the billions of dollars provided as Marshall Aid. And for decades afterwards, Abs had a powerful role in Germany. Until the mid-1990s, he was chairman of the Deutsche Bank.

When Hermann Abs died in 1994, he was remembered as a 'great man'. *The Independent*, a British newspaper, described Abs as the outstanding German banker of his time and quietly ignored his work with IG Farben and Kontinental-Ol where he had knowingly employed slave labour in the concentration camps. Nor did they mention the money he had helped steal from Jewish people and banks.

Konrad Adenauer (German 1876-1967)

On 20th September 1949, Konrad Adenauer, the first 'proper' post-War German Chancellor, made it clear that he intended to continue with Hitler's policies. (Technically, Goebbels was Chancellor for one day after Hitler's death.)

When he took office, as Germany's Chancellor, Adenauer announced: 'We shall continue along the road of the economic policies on which we have already successfully travelled.'

Adenauer was himself known to be a Nazi supporter and is regarded as an important figure in the history of the European Union. He is usually described as one of the 'leading founding fathers' of the EU and his attitude towards the Nazis is, therefore, extremely important.

You might imagine that Germany's first post-War Chancellor would take great care not to favour Nazis or to include Nazis in his government. In fact, no one could have done more than Adenauer to ensure that Nazis played an important part in the development of the 'new' Germany, and immediately after the end of the War, Adenauer deliberately allowed senior Nazis back into positions of great power. The fact that the EU still regards Adenauer as an important and respected figure tells us everything we need to know about the organisation's attitude towards Nazism.

Adenauer's Chief of Staff (Minister of the Chancellery) from 1953 to 1963 was a man called Hans Globke (qv).

Globke was a Nazi supporter who was involved in drafting the Nuremberg race laws, which revoked the German citizenship of Jews in 1935. Globke admitted that he knew that Jews were being killed in large numbers. (Globke had applied to be an official member of the Nazi party but had been turned down by Martin Bormann.)

As the most important man in Adenauer's post War Government, Globke was responsible for hiring men for senior appointments. (Adenauer, who had previously only been mayor of Cologne, was inexperienced and leant heavily on Globke.)

And so, thanks to Globke, the new secretary of state at the Ministry of German Affairs was Franz Thedieck, a man who had betrayed opponents of Nazism to the Gestapo. The secretary of state at the Finance Ministry was Alfred Hartmann, who had supervised the confiscation of Jewish property. The Ministry of Transport, the Ministry of Economics and so on and on were all in the hands of former Nazis. Many of Adenauer's appointees were Nazis with the worst records and when this was pointed out to him, the German Chancellor defended the appointments. Nazis were welcomed and protected by Adenauer.

As soon as Germany regained autonomy, Adenauer's new Government reversed Allied laws which had been introduced in 1948 in an attempt to introduce a little more democracy into the German civil service. Globke made changes which allowed former civil servants who had been removed from their positions because of their Nazi activities during the War to be returned to their positions (or to higher ones). The Nazis were back in power in Germany. Astonishingly, 184 former Nazi party members immediately returned to the Foreign Affairs Department. No fewer than 153 of these had worked under Ribbentrop. (Adenauer couldn't put Ribbentrop back into position because he had been executed.)

The Adenauer years were a bonanza for Nazis. In the early 1960s, according to Tom Bower, more than 60 West German ambassadors and foreign officers were former Nazi party members who had helped organise the Final Solution. There were former SS officers everywhere. Adenauer's personal assistant, a man called Herbert Blankenhorn, was a former Nazi but would in due course become an increasingly influential German diplomat. Almost unbelievably, the former Nazi was West German ambassador to the United Kingdom between 1965 and 1970. Prior to that, Blankenhorn had been West German ambassador to NATO, to France and to Italy.

It is inconceivable that Adenauer did not know what Globke had done during the War. And it is inconceivable that he did not know that Globke had restored the Nazis to power in Germany. It is however conceivable that he wholeheartedly approved of what had been done in his name.

Today, Adenauer, a committed supporter of Hitler and the Nazis, is regarded by the European Union as one of its founding fathers.

Karl Blessing (German 1900-1971)
Karl Blessing (see Abs) ended up being president of the Deutsche Bundesbank, the German Federal bank. During the War he was a close colleague and friend of Abs and other Nazi supporters and was a member of the Committee for Foreign Economic Affairs. Blessing was a close friend of Walther Funk and visited concentration camps with Himmler. He was an important member of the Third Reich.

Inevitably, the paperwork which might have resulted in him and his colleagues being imprisoned or executed was conveniently lost.

However, Blessing's proclamations of innocence were damaged when a letter came to light showing that in 1941 he asked to be given an apartment which the Gestapo had taken from a Jewish family.

Moreover, although Allen Dulles claimed that Blessing had not been a member of the Nazi party there is evidence that he had joined in 1937.

Blessing was one of the Nazis protected by Dulles so that he could play a part in helping to re-develop Germany and build the European Union. And so instead of being charged with War crimes, Blessing was freed and allowed to return to his old job at Unilever where he became a hugely well-paid executive. From there he went to join the Bundesbank. By this time Blessing had succeeded in cleansing his personal history and had remembered that during the War he had actually been a member of the Resistance and hadn't been a Nazi at all.

If he had lived just a little longer he would have doubtless claimed to have served in the British army.

Alexander Dolezalek (German 1914-1999)

Dolezalek was an SS officer who, during the War, headed an SS Department which existed solely to plan a united Europe. In other parts of the SS, officers worked on the 'Germanization' of conquered Europe. There were, for example, plans to make the German language obligatory and universal. Dolezalek planned to introduce a single European passport and to eliminate borders between countries within the 'new' European country. He planned that East Europeans would be regarded as 'second class humans'. After the War, Dolezalek did what many Nazis did: he changed his name and became someone else but carried on with the work he'd been doing in the Third Reich. And so Dolezalek became Bomhoff (he kept his first name) and was appointed head of the 'All-European educational project' and produced plans for a United States of Europe. Dolezalek, a committed Nazi and racist, was the first of the EU's founding fathers to describe the new Union as offering a means of ensuring lasting peace in Europe.

Allen Dulles (American 1893-1969)

Allen Dulles, was a lawyer, diplomat and administrator. In *Tower of Basel*, Adam Lebor writes that 'even as a precocious schoolboy he had shown an insatiable appetite for intrigue and geopolitics'. During World War II, Allen Dulles worked in Switzerland as a spymaster and served in the Office of Strategic Services (OSS), the forerunner of the Central Intelligence Agency (CIA). His brother John Foster Dulles was an eminent politician. Allen Dulles was close to Monnet (qv) and undoubtedly used him as an asset during the War.

The two Dulles brothers were both lawyers who had a number of rather dubious associations. Before the start of the Second World War, both brothers worked for a law firm which had associations with IG Farben.

Not surprisingly, neither brother is ever listed in the EU approved lists of founding fathers though there can be little doubt that both were responsible for putting into practice the American enthusiasm for the formation of a United States of Europe controlled by Germany.

After the War, Dulles protected many Nazis, helped them hide their pasts and arranged for them to be given high posts in the 'new' Germany (which, did not in truth, seem very different to the old one). He became the first chief of the Central Intelligence Agency.

John Foster Dulles (American 1888-1959)
John Foster Dulles was a lawyer and a politician.

After the First World War, JF Dulles helped design the Dawes Plan, which reduced the amount of money Germany had to pay in reparation and agreed a loan of $200 million from the United States. His sympathy for Germany continued after the Second World War.

He was Chief Foreign Policy adviser to Thomas E Dewey in the 1944 and 1948 elections.

When Eisenhower won the 1952 Presidential election, John Foster Dulles became Secretary of State from 1953 to 1959.

Both Dulles brothers appeared to have had powerful influence behind the scenes, helped to turn American policy into action and were instrumental in the development of the European Union.

Eisenhower (a former senior military officer) wanted to rid Europe of the Nazis and the Nazi influence, but many powerful

Americans, influenced by corporations which had huge business interests in Germany, were keen to ensure that Germany recovered quickly from the War and could lead the European Union which had been planned since the 1930s by Hitler and the Nazi party. They were helped by Americans such as Patton who believed that Russia was a major threat to Europe and could only be held back if a United States of Europe were created.

Throughout the War, John Foster Dulles wanted to maintain links with German industry so that business would not be interrupted at the end of the War. To achieve this end, Dulles worked with a number of people including Joseph Wallenberg, a Swedish businessman who had done a great deal of business with the Nazis during the War.

'We should seek the political reorganisation of continental Europe as a federated commonwealth,' said John Foster Dulles in 1941. 'This can be assured through federal principles, which in this respect are very flexible. But the re-establishment of some twenty five wholly independent sovereign states in Europe would be political folly.'

And so throughout the War, and immediately afterwards, the Americans did everything they could to expedite the formation of the European Union – with Germany in control.

Ludwig Erhard (German 1897-1977)

Ludwig Erhard, who took over the Chancellorship of West Germany after Adenauer, worked closely with Otto Ohlendorf who was a senior SS officer who had been head of a murder battalion which had executed 90,000 Russian civilians.

And so, the continuing Nazification of Germany, which Heinz Pol had warned about, continued long after the War as if nothing had happened.

The Nazis's plan for a new European Union which they controlled was carried out as efficiently as Funk, Ribbentrop and the others might have hoped.

Friedrich Flick (German 1883-1972)

Friedrich Flick, a steel manufacturer, coal-mine owner and director of Dresdener Bank, was one of the first industrialists to give money to the Nazis and to set them on their way. At a meeting at Goring's home in 1933, Flick had promised to give substantial sums to Hitler. He later gave vast sums to a special account held by Heinrich Himmler. During the War, Flick knowingly used slave labour in his mines. Perhaps inevitably, he claimed that the SS had forced him to employ the slave labour. (This was a widely used excuse. Unfortunately for Flick, evidence was produced which showed that he had demanded extra slave workers, complaining that he didn't have enough. He had 48,000 concentration camp workers.) Nevertheless, the judges at Nuremberg accepted that Flick was merely doing what he had been ordered to do. This defence was not accepted for SS officers or guards but, curiously, it was accepted for rich industrialists who had employed concentration camp inmates. No evidence was ever produced showing that industrialists who refused to use concentrate camp victims were punished in any way.

Flick was sentenced to seven years in prison but was pardoned shortly afterwards (as were most of the white collar Nazi war criminals). His wealth was not confiscated.

After the War, Flick sold his mines and with the money he had made during the War he became the largest shareholder in Daimler-Benz and bought large investments in a number of other companies. The Second World War, and his exploitation of slave labour, had made him Germany's richest man. Flick was reported to have made sure that Daimler-Benz employed only people who had been important in the Third Reich.

In subsequent years, Flick, a convicted war criminal, received a vast number of West German honours and became a significant figure in Germany and the developing European Union. At his death in 1972, he was reported to be the richest person in West Germany and one of the richest people in the world.

Walther Funk (German 1890-1960)
Funk was Hitler's Reich Economic Minister, and his speech 'The Economic Reorganisation of Europe' is the clear blueprint for the European Union as it exists today. Funk was one of relatively few

Nazis to have been imprisoned (though he, like most imprisoned Nazis, was released after serving a short sentence).

Funk's speech entitled 'The Economic Reorganisation of Europe' was delivered on July 25 in 1940, and in it the Fuhrer's economics guru outlined the Nazi's plans for the economic reorganisation of Europe in some detail. He spoke about a currency union and about how the new Germany would control Europe's future trade relations with Russia, South America, Asia and America. He concluded: 'A stronger sense of economic community among European nations must be aroused by collaboration in all spheres of economic policy (currency, credit, production, trade, etc.). The economic consolidation of European countries should improve their bargaining position in dealings with other economic groups in world economy. This united Europe will not submit to political and economic terms dictated to it by any extra-European body. It will trade on the basis of economic equality at all times in the knowledge of the weight which it carries in economic matters. The coming peace-time economy must guarantee for Greater Germany a maximum of economic security and for the German nation a maximum consumption of goods to raise the level of the nation's well-being. The European economy must be adapted to achieve this aim. Development will proceed by stages and differently in different countries; it is still beset with numerous uncertainties, for – we must never forget – we are still at war!'

In 1941, Walther Funk launched a plan which he called the Europaische Wirtschafts Gemeinschaft (European Economic Community). The aim of his EWG (EEC) was to integrate the European economy into a single market and to establish his idea for a single European currency. Funk recognised that it would be troublesome, even dangerous, to have a pan-European currency before there was complete political unity across Europe, but he knew that the existence of a single currency would make it easier to overcome opposition to federalisation and expedite the process of creating Hitler's United States of Europe.

The Nazis were so keen to create a new European Union that they formed a Society for European Economic Planning in Nazi Germany. The plan was to abolish the economic sovereignty of individual states and to create what Funk had called a 'European Economic Community'. The proposed EEC was defined precisely in

Nazi documents. The aim was for the Third Reich to take advantage of the countries it had conquered – replacing the sovereignty of the people with a super-state. The idea was that all the nations of Europe would work together to promote the development of the German economy. This is, of course, exactly what has happened.

The plan devised by the Nazis included the exploitation of weak peripheral countries such as Greece; the formation of European institutions which would be accountable only to the financial and industrial elite and not to the people of European countries; the positioning of the new EU in opposition to the Soviet Union; the elimination of national states within Europe; the centralisation of all economic and political power and the subjugation of all national interests to a unified Europe. All this is, of course, exactly how the modern European Union is organised and how it operates.

'European economic unity will come, for its time is here,' said Walther Funk in 1942.

In 1946, in a memo entitled 'Economic Reorganisation of Europe', Funk wrote that: 'There must be a readiness to subordinate one's own interests in certain causes to that of the European Community.' The document was immediately passed to Thomas McKittrick.

(It should be noted that it was six more years before a former OSS asset called Jean Monnet suggested the same thing. The difference, of course, is that Funk ended up as a war criminal in Spandau whereas Monnet did not – although Monnet himself appears to have had links with IG Farben during the War. Funk, who was the clear 'father' of the European Union, has been completely removed from the organisation's official history but Monnet is often described by Europhiles as yet another of the EU's founding fathers.)

Funk also wrote that 'the new European economy must be an organic growth' and that it would result from 'close economic collaboration between Germany and European countries'. Funk was wise enough to realise that the currency basis of post War Europe might not be the deutschmark itself but thought that this was of secondary importance to Germany maintaining economic leadership of the new, enlarged Germany. 'The currency problem will solve itself,' he wrote, 'because it will then be merely a question of suitable monetary technique.'

After the end of the War, Walther Funk, the main architect of the European Union and the man who should now be celebrated on all euro notes, was still alive but was one of the few civilian Nazis to end up in prison. He had simply been too close to Hitler, and too involved in the Nazi Government, to be allowed to remain free though, like most other Nazis, he claimed that he didn't really know what was going on, was simply following orders and wasn't responsible for any of the bad things that happened. (If you read the Nuremberg trials it soon becomes clear that there were no more than half a dozen 'real' Nazis in Germany – all the others were reluctantly obeying orders.)

Funk was released from prison after serving a few years of his sentence on the grounds that he did not feel well. (However, despite apparently not feeling well, Funk did not die until 1960.)

In 1988, Walther Funk's dream of a European currency began to show its first signs of life. As had been widely recommended, the whole process was shrouded in secrecy.

A special committee (the Committee for the Study of Economic and Monetary Union) was set up to prepare for the launch of the euro. One of the most influential members of the committee was Alexandre Lamfalussy, at the time the general director of the BIS; the central bank for central bankers, and the bank which had worked closely with the Nazis during the Second World War. It was decided that a new bank called the European Central Bank would be created to manage the new currency and the economies of those countries using the new currency. Further, it was decided that the European Central Bank (ECB) would be given complete independence and that the European Parliament (perhaps the weakest Parliament in history) would have no authority over the bank. The only organisation which has any influence or control over the ECB is, of course, the BIS – the secret bank, based in Switzerland, which helped the Nazis throughout the Second World War.

The BIS, the bank which, under Thomas McKittrick, handled the gold which the Nazis stole from millions of Jews, is now effectively controlling the economies of all EU member countries.

Finally, in 2002, just sixty years after Funk had published details of the new proposed pan-European currency, the euro was launched. The advantages, when listed, were identical to the advantages Walther Funk had outlined in 1940. To sell the new currency to an unwilling public, it was pointed out that holidaymakers travelling around Europe would find the new currency a great convenience and that they would be able to buy ice creams with the same currency in Germany, Italy and France. As Funk had predicted everyone in power within the EU knew (or should have known) that the new currency could not possibly work properly until the European Union had become the United States of Europe and individual nations had been lost in a new federal state.

Economists, politicians and commentators recognise that the euro has serious problems. They realise that the obvious mistake was to create the euro before completing the political unity which is a traditional pre-requirement for a currency. Some commentators seem surprised that (as the *Daily Telegraph* put it on 3rd January 2019): 'The euro crisis entrenched and amplified the power and influence of…Germany.'

What the economists perhaps fail to understand is that things are working out perfectly according to Funk's plans. For example, only belatedly are the economists realising that the 'rescue' of Greece was, in fact, merely a bailout designed to protect German banks.

Funk planned that the euro would have to come first – before the political unity – and he predicted that numerous problems would become apparent. It would be no surprise to him that the EU's policies have impoverished countries such as Italy and Greece and left Germany the sole economic winner. When these countries have attempted to defend themselves they have either been bullied into submission, or the elected politicians have simply been replaced by eurocrats.

Today, there are only two solutions: the countries within the Eurozone must either agree to the formation of a United States of Europe (something that would require France, Italy, Spain, Portugal, etc., to abandon what remains of their sovereignty) or they must abandon the euro.

There is very little public support for the former but the EU cannot and will not abandon the euro (however painful its maintenance becomes for the people of Europe) because the single currency was always a crucial part of Funk's long-term plan, and the descendants of the Nazi designers of the European Union now see complete and final victory within their grasp.

Hans Globke (German 1898-1973)

Hans Globke was a German lawyer and politician who helped direct the Nazi party towards the Holocaust. He worked with Adolf Eichmann and brought in many anti-semitic laws, including the one which revoked the citizenship of German Jews. He also helped organise the Holocaust.

It was Globke who was responsible for insisting that all Jews in Hitler's Germany were to be named Israel or Sara so that they could be easily identified by the authorities. It was thanks to Globke that half a million Germans were faced with discriminatory laws. Globke's laws were so highly thought of that they were used in Austria, Czechoslovakia and throughout German controlled Europe. Adolf Eichmann described Globke's work as 'basic for the Final Solution of the Jewish people'.

At the end of the War, however, Globke did what most of the guilty Germans did: he blamed everything on dead Nazis and denied everything. And, amazingly, his denials were accepted. He was briefly imprisoned but then released.

Globke was not unique. In his book *Blind Eye to Murder*, Tom Bower estimates that 250,000 Germans were directly involved in Nazi murders. Of these, just over 35,000 were convicted of war crimes. The other 215,000 were allowed to go free, often obtaining powerful and influential positions in the post-war Germany and the developing European Union. In *The Hidden Enemy*, Heniz Pol estimated that the Gestapo and Labour Front organisations each had at least 50,000 to 75,000 members and that there were at least another 50,000 to 75,000 organisers and teachers for the SS and the Peasant Front. Altogether, he estimated that there were up to 200,000 full-fledged and wholehearted Nazis in Germany. Most of them went unpunished at the end of the War and took positions of power and influence in the new Germany and the developing European Union.

At the Nuremberg trials, Globke appeared as a witness for both the prosecution and the defence and admitted that he knew that Jews were being murdered en masse.

However, the Americans considered him to be too important and useful to be tried and immediately after the War he became one of the most powerful people in the German Government. He ensured that the German Government and the civil service were packed with former Nazis and he became Germany's main liaison with NATO and the CIA. The Americans protected Globke after the War – even insisting that references to Globke be removed from Eichmann's memoirs.

After he retired, Globke wanted to retire to Switzerland but the Swiss denied him entry – wisely labelling him an 'unwanted foreigner'.

Paul Joseph Goebbels (German 1897-1945)
Goebbels was a Nazi politician and Reich Minister of Propaganda from 1933 to 1945.

Goebbels was a devout believer in the development of a new European Union, under the control of Germany, and for many years, he devoted huge amounts of space in the German newspaper *Das Reich* to articles about 'the new Europe' and 'the vision of a new Europe'. Goebbels was an extraordinarily efficient propagandist whose techniques of indoctrination, misdirection and misinformation are today practised to great effect by both the European Union itself and, in the United Kingdom, the British Broadcasting Corporation.

Hermann Goring (German) 1893-1946
Now largely remembered for stealing art treasures from Jews and for setting fire to the Reichstag (something which he admitted at Hitler's birthday party in 1942 and which was reported at the Nuremberg trials by General Franz Halder who had been there). The Nazis used the fire to help them pretend that the communists were trying to take over Germany and the burning of the Reichstag is regarded as a classic 'false flag' action.

Goring was one of the most powerful Nazis and the creator of the Gestapo. He was the second most powerful man in Germany and the senior army officer. He was closely involved in all economic affairs, including plans for the European Union.

Hermann Goring, had set up a company called Kontinental-Ol to take advantage of oil supplies in central Europe and the Balkans (Blessing soon became a director of that company too). Kontinental-

Ol's money was supplied by Deutsche Bank, through Hermann Abs (qv).

As with IG Farben, Goring's company made its money through murder, theft and slavery and was one of the Third Reich's biggest uses of concentration camp inmates. There was a constant need for new workers since the average life expectation of employees was three to six months. When Kontinental-Ol shut down its camps at the end of the War, the inmates of the camps were shot to stop them talking.

Charles Higham, writing in his meticulously researched book *Trading with the Enemy*, revealed that Goring had close relationships with a number of American companies.

Friedrich Grimm (German 1888-1959)

Friedrich Grimm, who had joined the Nazi party in 1933 had, in 1936, published a book entitled *Hitler and Europe*. He became vice-president of the Deutsch-Franzosische Gesellschaft in 1937.

Grimm argued that France and Germany should combine to save Europe from Bolsheviks and Jews. He spent much of the War promoting the idea of a 'new European order'. Today, he is described as a 'convinced European' who played an important part in the development of the European Union.

Walter Hallstein (German 1901-1982)

Hallstein was the father of European Law in the 1930s and 1940s and was a member of the National Socialist Union of Jurists. During the Second World War, while working as a Nazi, Hallstein used legal phrases and proposals (designed for controlling occupied countries) which he later used when preparing European Law for the European Union. Hallstein was the first president of the Commission of the European Economic Community and the European Union, unable to erase him from their history, now recognises him as one of the founding fathers of the EU.

On January 23, 1939, Walter Hallstein, who was Dean of the Faculty of Law and Economics at the University of Rostock, in Germany, gave a propaganda speech about the restructuring of Europe. The speech was part of the preparation for war by the Nazi regime and their powerful partners the oil and drug cartel IG Farben. The Nazis had already annexed Austria and the Czech territories of Bohemia and Moravia, and in his speech Hallstein describes the planned German conquest of the rest of Europe and the subjugation of the continent. In due course, Hallstein became an officer in the German army. In 1938, Hallstein had been part of the official Nazi delegation to Rome.

Hallstein was jointly responsible for writing a document which included this section: 'The legal order of the dictatorial state (Greater Germany) has the task to protect the integrity, the health and the racial health of its people…The supreme race has to be particularly protected from the Jewish race by eliminating it from society for all time.'

In 1957, Walter Hallstein (who had always been a keen federalist, with the aim of Germany controlling Europe) returned to Rome as one of the signatories of the EU's 'Treaty of Rome' and in the same year became the first president of the commission of the European Economic Community. It was Hallstein who was the architect of the now enormously powerful EU Commission (the politburo of the EU).

Hallstein later wrote a book called *Europe in the Making* in which he described the role of the EU commissioners. Here is a quote: 'The Commission is entrusted with what virtually amounts to a monopoly in taking the initiative in all matters affecting the Community. There are a few exceptions to this general rule, but these ought to be removed at the earliest opportunity. As I see it the Commission should eventually be empowered to take all measures necessary for the implementation of the Treaty on its own authority, without having to rely on special and specific approval by the Council of Ministers. Furthermore, the big and small policy decisions, by which the Commission, and the Commission alone, must at present exercise its executive authority, will in some way have to be relaxed. This could be done by giving the different departments of the Commission under their Directors-General greater responsibility or by setting up separate agencies. The departments or the agencies would of course continue to act under the general supervision of the Commission for approval in every case.'

This is, of course, exactly what has happened. Hallstein's plan for the management of the European Union has been followed to the letter.

Hallstein has been accurately described as the 'Founding Father of the Brussels EU'. The EU does not mention Hallstein's links to the Nazis or his work with IG Farben. Nor does the EU mention their founding father's determination to eliminate the Jewish race and today there is no published evidence that eradicating the Jewish race is official EU policy although, of course, there is also no published evidence that it isn't.

Adolf Hitler (Austrian 1889-1945)

It would be entirely unfair not to include Adolf Hitler as one of the founding fathers of the European Union. It was his ambition and drive which led the way to the creation of what he liked to call the 'United States of Europe'. 'The construction of a new Europe belongs to us,' said Hitler at the start of the Second World War. By 1940, he was confident enough to announce that: 'Germany has given freedom to the European continent.'

Lutz Graf Schwerin Von Krosigk (German 1887-1977)

After the death of Adolf Hitler, Joseph Goebbels became Chancellor of Germany for one day. And after Goebbels death, the next temporary Chancellor was Lutz Graf Schwerin von Krosigk. Astonishingly, von Krosigk, who was a member of the Nazi party, had also been a member of Hitler's cabinet. He was responsible for the persecution of Jews in Germany and other European countries. He also stole their property and laundered money. In 1949, he was convicted of war crimes and sentenced to ten years in jail. However, in 1951, his sentence was commuted by Konrad Adenauer (the Chancellor who claimed that he hadn't been a Nazi, though he arranged for Nazi flags to be flown, helped the Nazis in other ways and hired a Nazi as his Chief of Staff).

Alfried Krupp (Alfried Krupp von Bohlen und Halbach) (German 1907-1967)

In 1942, Alfried Krupp, the eponymous head of one of Germany's biggest companies, was having difficulty finding enough workers to make armaments and so in May of that year Krupp approached Hitler and Himmler and suggested a solution. He thought a contract between Krupp and the SS to use concentrate camp inmates would benefit everyone. Krupp could obtain the labour he needed and the Krupp factories would pay the SS a daily rate for the workers. Himmler thought this a splendid idea. But the supply of slave workers was still insufficient and so Krupp approached Rudolf Hoess, the commandant of Auschwitz with another idea. He wanted to build a Krupp factory inside the extermination camp and to use the people in his private camp in his factory. Unfortunately, for Krupp the deal didn't work well because Hoess preferred gassing prisoners rather than putting them to work. (Hoess, not being rich or well-connected, was hung after his trial at Nuremberg and so played no part in the development of the EU.)

Frustrated by Hoess, Krupp did deals with everyone else he could find who was prepared to send him concentration camp inmates. Even children as young as six-years-old were forced to work in Krupp's factories. If they didn't work hard enough they didn't receive any food. (The 'food' being a once a day 350 calorie bowl of soup.) Throughout the War, no one exploited concentration camp slaves as efficiently or as profitably as Alfried Krupp. Even when it was clear that the War had been lost, Krupp continued to make young prisoners (including children) work in brutal conditions in his factories.

Being much richer than Hoess, and having more powerful friends, Krupp, who had been sentenced to 12 years imprisonment at Nuremberg, was released by the American McCloy after just three years in prison. It is worth recording that Krupp's imprisonment does not sound much like punishment. A room in the prison was been set aside so that the Krupp directors could discuss corporate business and Alfried was supplied with the best food and wines available and apparently took delight in insulting the people who had been responsible for his incarceration.

Incredibly, McCloy even arranged for Krupp to be pardoned and his record as a war criminal expunged.

Krupp's industrial empire had controlled slave labourers in 57 concentration camps. Krupp, who was also Hitler's Minster of

Armament and War Production was close to Hitler and was responsible for transferring factories from occupied territories to the German Reich. He was one of the most evil members of the Nazi regime and was awarded medals by Hitler for keeping up production of arms through the use of slave labour.

McCloy later explained his pardon for Krupp by claiming that the German was a 'playboy' who had not had much responsibility. In fact, Krupp had been very much a hands-on operator and running the companies had been entirely his responsibility.

Astonishingly, McCloy even ordered that all of Krupp's property, which had been confiscated after the War, be restored to him so that he suffered not at all.

After his release and pardon, Krupp, one of the richest and worst German war criminals, quickly became a seemingly 'respectable' German citizen accepted by German society and playing an important part in the enriching of Germany and the development of the European Union.

Prince Bernhard of Lippe-Biesterfled (German 1911-2004)
Prince Bernhard of Lippe-Biesterfled in Germany was a keen supporter of a federal Europe. (Bernhard later married Crown Princess Juliana of the Netherlands.) Bernhard was a Nazi member and also a member of the SS but curiously he is usually omitted from lists of the EU's founding fathers. He was, however, one of the most important figures in the development of the EU.

In 1954, Bernhard sponsored the first meeting of European federalists and their American supporters at the Bilderberg Hotel in the Netherlands. (The promotion of a federal Europe, or United States of Europe, has always been the main reason for the secretive annual Bilderberg conferences.) In 1955, the delegates at the Bilderberg conference planned to create a European Union with a single currency – as had been originally described by Walther Funk and other Nazis.

The Bilderbergers (as they like to call themselves) still meet regularly and secretly and attendees are usually enthusiastic supporters of the European Union.

John McCloy (American 1895-1989)

McCloy, a former president of the World Bank, had been a partner in a law firm which represented the American portion of IG Farben and subsequently acquire a reputation for having sympathy for the Nazis. Much of what he did now seems inexplicable.

Early in the War, McCloy used his influence to block attempts by Jewish organisations to persuade the US Air Force to bomb Auschwitz because he knew how crucial the concentration camp was to German Industry. It was known that it would have been easy for bombers to destroy the gas chambers and key railway junctions but McCloy (who was, at the time, the Assistant Secretary of War) claimed that bombing Auschwitz might annoy the Germans and provoke them into vindictive actions. Some found it difficult to understand precisely what 'vindictive actions' he had in mind.

It was, however, McCloy's actions after the War which helped create the European Union.

After the War, McCloy became US High Commissioner for West Germany. In addition to releasing many industrialists who had been sentenced to prison, he also arranged for Nazi camp doctors and SS officers to be released or to have their sentences substantially reduced.

As soon as McCloy had arranged for their release, the executives from IG Farben quickly re-joined German companies, with, for example, Schmitz joining the board of Deutsche Bank.

McCloy was never subjected to serious criticism for any of his actions because he was obeying American instructions. Although President Eisenhower had wanted to rid Germany of the influence of the Nazis, there were other powerful Americans who felt differently. Allen Dulles, John Foster Dulles and General Patton all wanted the Germans to control Europe as a bulwark against the Soviet Union.

After the War, McCloy served as chairman of the Chase Manhattan Bank and the Ford Foundation. Thomas McKittrick also became a director of Chase Manhattan; a bank which had had strong links with the Nazis during the War. McCloy also became chairman of the Council on Foreign Relations and an adviser to five American Presidents.

In 1963, the man who had worked with the manufacturer of the gas which had been used to murder millions of Jews and who had ordered the early release of some of Germany's worst war criminals, was presented with the Presidential Medal of Freedom by President Lyndon B Johnson.

It was entirely thanks to the efforts of people such as McCloy and McKittrick that Schmitz, Krupp and other war criminals (who were as responsible as Hitler, Himmler et al for the horrors of the Second World War and the efficient brutality of the Nazi war machine) received no punishment at all or the sort of punishment usually regarded as suitable for small time motoring offenders. It was released war criminals who helped found the European Union.

Thomas McKittrick (American 1889-1970)

McKittrick was an American banker and President of the Bank for International Settlements. He had a close relationship with Adolf Hitler and was a Nazi sympathiser.

McKittrick used the Bank for International Settlements to help the Nazis steal money and use it for their War effort.

After the War the odious McKittrick (who was never charged with War crimes) became a director of Chase National Bank. This is not surprising since the Chase National Bank also had close links to the Nazis during World War II. The bank had enabled Nazi sympathisers in America to buy dollars at a discounted rate. To do this the Chase National Bank handled money which had been stolen from Jews who had fled from Germany. The Chase National Bank is believed to have earned $500,000 in commission for this work. No one from the Bank was ever prosecuted 'in the interests of national security'.

In 1970, Thomas McKittrick died at the age of 81. *The New York Times* described him as a 'world financier'. There was no mention of looted gold or secret deals with the Nazis.

Jean Monnet (French 1888-1979)

In 1944, Jean Monnet wrote a memo in which he said: 'Prosperity and vital social progress will remain elusive until the nations of Europe form a federation of a 'European entity' which will force them into a single economic unit.'

Monnet was an asset of Allan Dulles, the OSS representative in Europe and has been described as Roosevelt's eyes and ears in

Europe. For reasons explained elsewhere, the Americans were keen to see a European Union develop. Monnet was a mover and shaker, someone who would today be known as an efficient networker, and he believed that the technocrats should rule – without being disturbed by the will of the people.

In 1946, Jean Monnet began to plan the European project which he had drawn up with John Foster Dulles and which had been originally devised by Walther Funk, Ribbentrop et al. Monnet is today talked about as one of the fathers of the European Union. Those who talk of him in this way do not usually mention that Monnet had been associated with the dishonourable McKittrick and appears to have had links with IG Farben – the owner of a concentration camp at Auschitz and the manufacturer of the gas used in the gas chambers. Monnet was almost certainly an agent for the OSS and his influence depended upon his links with the Dulles brothers and John McCloy. (Mysteriously, much paperwork disappeared towards the end of the War.) A less well connected man might have found himself enjoying a starring role at the Nuremberg trials.

Oswald Moseley (British 1896-1980)
Oswald Moseley, the fascist leader, spent much time after the War campaigning for European integration. In 1953, he founded a magazine called *The European* and in 1958 he published a book entitled *Europe: Faith and Plan – A Way Out from the Coming Crises and an Introduction to Thinking as a European.*

Moseley was an enthusiastic supporter of the developing European Union (which he recognised as a uniquely fascist organisation) and he should be included among the EU's list of founding fathers. It was Moseley who first talked of 'large trading blocks' and 'a common agricultural policy' – ideas and phrases later adopted by the European Union as its own.

Emmanuel Mournier (French 1905-1950)
Emmanuel Mounier, a fascist, a keen Nazi supporter, a lifelong supporter of a federal Europe and an opponent of parliamentarianism and capitalism, had great influence on the continent of Europe.

In 1936, Mournier attended a summer camp with the Hitler Youth movement and wrote that 'communitarian feeling was one of the most exciting psychological aspects of the Nazi vision of the world'. (In 1982, Helmut Kohl was elected Chancellor Germany. Kohl, too, had been sworn into the Hitler Youth movement – a first step towards being a Nazi.)

According to John Laughland, in his magnificently researched book *The Tainted Source*, Mounier 'was fascinated by Nazism'. He was also enthusiastic about fascism. Mounier wrote of the 'authentic spiritual vigour' which he felt the Nazis possessed.

After France surrendered to the Nazis, Mounier became actively involved in the Vichy 'government' under Marshall Petain.

Today, Mounier is usually described as the spiritual godfather of the European movement. Naturally, his relationship with the Nazis is omitted from officially approved biographies.

Benito Mussolini (Italian 1883-1945)

Benito Mussolini, the inventor of fascism, was an enthusiastic supporter of the idea of a European Union. He was Prime Minister of Italy from 1922 to 1943 and Duce of the Italian Social Republic from 1943 to 1945.

Surprisingly, Mussolini's political career began when he was hired by the British Secret Service (with a fee in excess of £6,000 a week in today's money) to publish propaganda.

Like all of the EU's creators, Mussolini did not believe in democracy. He preferred a police state and (again, like the EU) preferred to control the people through propaganda.

By the late 1930s, Mussolini had decided that Britain and France were finished and that Italy and Germany were destined to rule Europe together. Under Mussolini's leadership, Italy joined Germany in the War against Britain in 1940. The aim was to create a pan-European state with Germany as the senior partner.

Mussolini is not listed by the EU as one of its official founding fathers.

Montagu Norman (1871-1950)

During the War, Montagu Norman helped the Nazis steal gold from the banks of countries which they had occupied. He must have known that the gold was being used to finance the Nazi War machine and to prepare Germany to control Europe – whatever the outcome of the War. Norman, who was proud of being a currency manipulator, helped create the Bank for International Settlements for the Nazis and was a close friend of Schacht (qv). After the War, instead of being arrested as a war criminal, he was made Baron Norman of St Clere and given the Distinguished Service Order.

General George S Patton Jr (American 1885-1945)
After the end of the War it was Patton who disobeyed Eisenhower's instruction that Germany be 'denazified'. Patton, the highest ranking and most powerful American in Europe, was worried that without the Nazis in position, Germany would be controlled by communists. It was Patton, therefore, who helped ensure that post war Germany was run by Nazis who continued with Hitler's aim of developing a United States of Europe controlled by Germany.

Major Vidkun Quisling (Norwegian 1887-1945)
Major Vidkun Quisling was a Norwegian army officer and diplomat who ruled Norway on behalf of the German occupying forces during 1940-1945. He was an enthusiastic supporter of the Nazis and their plans and was shot as a traitor in 1945. In accordance with Nazi guidelines, he believed that Europe would be strong and peaceful only if united. 'We must create a Europe that does not squander its blood and strength in internecine conflict, but forms a compact unity,' he wrote in an article entitled 'Norway and the Germanic Task in Europe' which was published in 1942. 'In this way it will become richer, stronger and more civilised, and will recover its old place in the world.' Quisling also said that: 'the interests and needs of Germany are essentially and inseparably linked with those of Europe'.

There is an endless amount of evidence to show that the Nazis promoted the idea of a European Union in Norway. Major Quisling said: 'We must create a Europe that does not squander its blood and strength in internecine conflict, but forms a compact unity. In this way it will become richer, stronger and more civilised and will recover its old place in the world.'

In view of his stance on pan European politics (he stated that there was no opposition between European economic cooperation and National Socialism) he could reasonably expect to be regarded as one of the founding fathers of the European Union, though curiously the EU never seems to list him with the other Nazis and Nazi supporters when producing their chosen list of founding fathers. He does not have a building, a square or even a telephone kiosk named after him in Brussels. His name is, however, to be found in most dictionaries and is used to describe a traitor who collaborates with an enemy force occupying their country.

Joachim von Ribbentrop (German 1893-1946)
Ribbentrop's office at the Ministry of Foreign Affairs worked on draft documents for a United Europe. After Germany's defeat at Stalingrad, Ribbentrop and the SS put extra effort into their plans for the new, expanded Germany. Ribbentrop, who was Hitler's Foreign Minister, felt it was necessary to mobilise the population of Europe against the threat of the Soviet Union.

In 1942, the Reich Ministry of Foreign Affairs began work on a new European Committee and Goebbels' Propaganda Office issued a communique which called for a new European image of German foreign policy. On 21st March 1942, Ribbentrop sent a note to Adolf Hitler in which he remarked that there was need for a new European Confederation to include Germany, Italy, France, Denmark, Norway, Finland, Slovakia, Hungary, Romania, Bulgaria, Croatia, Serbia, Greece and Spain.

On March 21, in 1943, Ribbentrop proposed the formation of a European Confederation. The Germans were by this time concerned about the growing might of the Soviet Union and felt that a United Europe would make Germany better able to combat USSR. Ribbentrop suggested abolishing customs barriers between all those countries. (The Americans had the same idea and their enthusiasm for the European Union was in part a response to their fear of the USSR.)

A few months later, on September 9th 1943, the Ministry proposed precise details for the new European Confederation. The plans were pretty well identical to the current structure of the European Union. There were proposals for a European Central Bank, European Monetary Union and a European Economic Council. The European Union has followed the Third Reich's proposals to the letter.

In June of the same year, a Nazi official submitted the 'Basic Elements of a Plan for the New Europe' to the committee. The paper suggested that Europeans should have a customs union, favouring trade between countries within Confederation. It also repeated Funk's earlier proposals for European monetary union and the harmonisation of labour conditions and social welfare. It even suggested the formation of separate 'conferences' for all individual areas – such as Labour and Agriculture – and proposed that the bureaucrats working in these 'conferences' should decide policy for the whole Confederation. An official in the Nazi ministry of employment declared that Germany was not fighting for herself but for Europe. And it was declared that 'Every continental state must remain conscious of its responsibility towards the European Economic Community'.

The plan proposed by Ribbentrop and his colleagues is, of course, identical to the way that the European Union operates. The only difference is that the European Union uses the term 'commissions' rather than 'conferences'.

Ribbentrop suggested that a new European currency be known as European Monetary Union and that a European Central Bank be created. These names are used today by the European Union. The Third Reich plan was that the other nations of Europe would help promote the development of the German economy. This is, of course, exactly what has happened through the modern European Union.

Ribbentrop should be listed as a major founder of the European Union.

Gustaw Schlotterer (German 1906-1989)

Schlotterer was an SS officer and Secretary of State of the Imperial Ministry of Economy under Hitler. He proposed building a unified, integrated Europe and suggested linking national economies to further German interests. Schlotterer put together a Commission (the Schlotterer Commission) which drew up plans for a European Bank. The Schlotterer Commission's plan was supported by German steel and coal business leaders of the Ruhr who later helped form the European Coal and Steel Community. Former Nazis became enthusiastic advocates of the new 'European Idea'.

The powerful German industrialists who had helped Hitler to power initiated the creation of the European Coal and Steel Community. After the end of the Second World War, SS officer Schlotterer, who had been secretary of state at the Imperial Ministry of Economy, obtained work as an economist working for the steel industry.

It was Schlotterer who drew up plans for the future European Central Bank. (The term 'European Economic Community', a title which was later used by the developing European Union, had already been suggested by Walther Funk and the economic department of the Third Reich.)

Other German planners wrote of the need to improve European railways, roads and airlines in accordance with a common plan. Half a century later, this became official EU policy.

It was also the Nazis who were first to recommend the introduction of a single European passport.

Hans-Ernst Schneider (German 1909-1999)

At the end of the War, many Nazis simply took off their uniforms, threw away their identification papers and changed identities. Some were very successful in creating new lives for themselves. So, for example, consider a Nazi SS officer called Hans-Ernst Schneider who had served on Heinrich Himmler's staff. Schneider was the leader of a unit which carried horrific experiments on concentration camp inmates but after the War he obtained documents 'proving' that he was Hans Schwerte, an ordinary soldier.

During the years which followed, the newly born Schwerte became an eminent academic and was given many honours by German and Belgian authorities. Only when he was threatened with exposure in 1995 did the 87-year-old Schwerte come clean and admit that he had been one of the very worst Nazis.

The significance of Schneider/Schwerte is two-fold.

First, his career illustrates just how efficiently the Nazis were at abandoning their past and re-establishing themselves in German life.

Second, when he had been an SS officer, Schneider/Schwerte had been working on Funk's idea of developing a new Europe. On March 1st 1945, he was told to develop the idea of European integration. Unfortunately, the timing wasn't terribly good and within a couple of months the Germans had surrendered to the Allies. This did not, however, prove to be much of a drawback for Schneider who disappeared completely and then reappeared with documents proving that his name was Hans Schwerte. The newly minted Schwerte got a job with a publishing company which was busily producing propaganda promoting European integration and the 'European idea'. At the same time that they hired Schwerte, the publisher also hired a number of other former Nazi officers who were doing exactly the same work that they had all been doing for the Third Reich. Here is more proof that the Nazis had very effectively succeeded in continuing with their plan for a federal Europe.

Although the organisation declared itself to be 'left-liberal' in its leanings, the plan was to create a new Europe, as a geopolitical entity which would, of course, be dominated by Germany and which would be avowedly anti-Communist. These plans delighted the United States of America which wanted to use the former Nazis to create a new European entity which could stand up to Russia. The Americans did not care that the plans were being devised by Nazis and, indeed, there is clear evidence (described elsewhere in this book) that a number of powerful Americans worked with senior Nazis during the Second World War, protected them from punishment at Nuremberg and helped them create the new Germany-dominated Europe.

Hjalmar Horace Greeley Schacht (German 1877-1970)

Schacht was a member of Hitler's government and President of the German Central Bank (the Reichsbank). He was a strong supporter of Hitler and the Nazi party. In 1938, Schacht suggested that Hitler should confiscate Jewish property in Germany but hold it in trust and used as security for loans from abroad. He also suggested that money should be given to emigrating Jews in order to overcome the objections of countries which would not accept penniless Jews. In 1943, he was dismissed from the Nazi Government after being accused of involvement in the attempt on Hitler's life. He was tried at Nuremberg but although the Russian judges wanted to convict him he was fully acquitted. He then founded a private bank and advised developing countries on economic development.

Both Gunston, a manager of the Bank of England, and Sir Montagu Norman, the director of the Bank of England, were strong supporters of Hjalmar Schacht and helped protect him after the War. Norman was godfather to one of Schacht's grandchildren. Both Schacht and Norman were directors of the BIS during the War.

Hermann Schmitz (German1881-1960)

Schmitz was a powerful figure at IG Farben. In 1929 Schmitz, together with Edsel Ford and Walter Teagle of Standard Oil (the oil company which helped the Nazis in World War Two) and one or two others set up the American edition of IG Farben. Throughout the Second World War, Edsel Ford and his father Henry both worked closely with the Nazis. According to Charles Higham, they refused to build aircraft engines for Britain but instead built military trucks for the Nazis. (Ford was not alone in this. General Motors built trucks, tanks and armoured cars for Nazi Germany in the 1930s and was, astonishingly, given $33 million tax exemption after the end of the War on the grounds that its airplane and vehicle factories in Germany had been damaged by bombing during World War II.) Ford would invariably send Hitler a generous birthday gift each year. In 1941, Henry Ford gave an interview to the *Manchester Guardian* in which he stated that the US should force England and Germany to fight until they both collapsed and that after that the two countries should join together in a coalition.

Schmitz was the president of IG Farben and in 1930 he met President Herbert Hoover and the two men found that they shared a fear and hatred of Russia. It was this fear of Russia which would later lead the Americans to push for the formation of the European

Union – an organisation which they hoped would be a powerful European barrier to Soviet progress.

In Germany, IG Farben was by far the most important company. It produced a vast range of products including oils, rubber, nylon, plastic, chemicals and a range of poison gases (including the gas which was used at the company's combination rubber factory and concentration camp at Auschwitz).

Schmitz was a founder member of the Bank for International Settlements and stayed on the board until the end of World War II. It was with Schmitz's help that the Nazis could grow in power for IG Farben provided the Nazis with most of the military and commercial goods they required – as well as millions of dollars' worth of foreign exchange. Schmitz was close to another director of the BIS called Kurt von Schroder – who was a dedicated Nazi and a leader of the Death's Head Brigade of the SS. It was Schroder who, with a group of associates, gave a million marks a year to Himmler.

At the end of the War, Schmitz was imprisoned but thanks to many powerful friends he was not seriously punished for his part in the deaths of many millions of Jews at Auschwitz. He was sentenced to four years in prison for 'war crimes and crimes against humanity' and was released in 1950. He was not required to give back the huge amounts of money he had made out of Auschwitz. After his release he was appointed to the administrators' council of Deutsche Bank and made honorary president of 'Rheinische Stahlwerke AG'.

Robert Schuman (Luxembourg 1886-1963)

Robert Schuman was a member of Paul Reynaud's wartime government in France, in charge of refugees. When France surrendered to the Nazis, Schuman kept his post under the Petain government and on 10th July 1940, Schuman pledged allegiance to Adolf Hitler and voted to give full power to Marshall Petain – who supported Hitler. At the end of the War, Marshall Petain was convicted of treason. He was originally sentenced to death as a Nazi collaborator but his sentence was commuted to life in prison.

In June 1944, Robert Schuman, the Secretary of State of Vichy France, stated: 'We will help Germany on every front and in every way to preserve the West, its enlightenment, its culture, its traditions.'

Robert Schuman, later described as a founding father of the EU, had supported the surrender of France to Hitler, the Third Reich and Nazi Germany and had supported the formation of Marshall Petain's government. Normally, a War time history as a quisling would have resulted in an appearance at one of the Nuremberg trials but Schuman was a committed enthusiast for the development of a European Union and was, therefore, invaluable to other Nazis and the Americans. He was not hung and not imprisoned. Indeed, although he was a known Nazi supporter, he was never arrested or charged (though he was vilified as a 'Vichy product who should be kicked out').

Before and during the War, Schuman spoke about the need for some sort of arrangement between France and Germany.

Schuman, an enthusiastic Nazi supporter, created the European Coal and Steel Community (which developed into the European Union) and is today described as one of the founding fathers of the European Union.

Arthur Seyss-Inquart (Austria 1892-1946)
Arthur Seyss-Inquart, the Nazi ruler of the occupied Netherlands, suggested that there was a need for a new European community and claimed that there would inevitably be an increase in prosperity when national barriers had been removed. He was following his leader for Hitler had already called for the removal of what he called a clutter of small nations. Seyss-Inquart was hung in October 1946 and is usually completely airbrushed from the EU's history.

Franz Alfred Six (German 1909-1975)
In 1942, the German Foreign Ministry founded a 'Europe Committee', consisting of officials from the Foreign Ministry and the Institute for the Study of Foreign Countries. The committee's most important member was Franz Alfred Six. Herr Six was a Nazi official who was appointed by Reinhard Heydrich, rose to the rank of SS Brigadefuhrer and created six death squads in the UK which

were charged with eliminating civilian resistance members and Jews all over Great Britain.

At the Nuremberg trials in 1948, Six was sentenced to 20 years imprisonment but inexplicably he was released in 1952 and went to work as a publicity executive for Porsche.

Altiero Spinelli (Italian 1907-1986)

Altiero Spinelli, a former communist, attended a meeting held in Milan in 1943 where it was proposed that a European federation be created. Altiero Spinelli was a committed Euro-federalist and is now recognised as (yet) another of the many officially recognised founding fathers of the EU. The EU's eurocrats like to have several founding fathers so that they can answer criticism that such and such a founding father was a Nazi.

The main building of the European Parliament in Brussels is named after Spinelli who, following the Nazi plan, wanted a United States of Europe with its own Armed Forces and its own constitution.

Like all the other official founding fathers of the EU Spinelli had no interest in democracy and did not believe that the people of Europe should be involved in the design or management of the new European super-state.

Alberto Di Stefani (Italian 1879-1969)

Alberto Di Stefani, who was a keen fascist and Mussolini's finance minister, was an enthusiastic supporter of the EU. He wrote: 'A European Union could not be subject to the variations of internal policy that are characteristic of liberal regimes.'

Fritz Thyssen (German 1873-1951)

At the Nuremberg trials, Fritz Thyssen, a rich and powerful German businessman, was tried for being a supporter of the Nazi party. In the 1920s and1930s, Thyssen made huge donations to Hitler and Thyssen himself claimed to have donated one million marks to the Nazi party. He joined the Nazi party in 1933, and accepted the exclusion of Jews from German life. He dismissed his own Jewish employees.

When the War ended, Thyssen inevitably denied involvement in the employment of slave labour.

(In 1945, Germany was full of ex Nazis who denied having anything to do with the Third Reich, either blaming people who were dead or claiming that, if they had done anything bad, then it was because they had been forced to do so. It is surprising just how few Nazis there appear to have been during the War. Indeed, it sometimes seems that Hitler must have fought the Second World War pretty well by himself – with just a few unwilling conscripts being forced to run the concentration camps.)

Thanks to his pleading, Thyssen was not imprisoned for his crimes but was fined a relatively modest 15% of his assets. (I describe this as a modest percentage since much of his wealth had been accumulated during the War, from working with the Nazis.)

Thyssen quickly ran away to Argentina, with thousands of other Nazis, presumably relieved to have got off so lightly and eager to be beyond extradition if anyone changed their minds. Money which the Nazis took to Argentina was used to help the Nazis maintain influence in Germany and to help develop the European Union.

(Incidentally, when I checked the Wikipedia entry for the thyssenkrupp conglomerate I found that it dismissed the Wartime activities of Thyssen and Krupp in a short paragraph, mentioning that labour was supplemented by 'foreign workers, forced labourers and prisoners of war'. There is no mention that these were concentration camp inmates – with a life expectation of just a few months. And there is no mention of Auschwitz. Nor is there any mention of six-year-olds being forced to work until they dropped. And then being gassed.)

Ludger Westrick (German 1894-1990)
Ludger Westrick became a Secretary of State in the Ministry of Economics in West Germany under Konrad Adenaeur (himself a recognised Nazi supporter qv). Westrick had, with Abs (qv) been a member of a secret group which met during the War to plan German domination of Europe when the War finally ended.

Karl Wurster (German 1900-1974)

Karl Wurster, who had joined the Nazi party in 1937, had served with a right-wing militia between the First and Second World Wars. In 1947, he was arrested to face trial at Nuremberg.

During the War, Wurster had been a director of IG Farben and had coordinated the company's work with the Nazis. Wurster had actually been chairman of a subsidiary which had made the gas used in the gas chambers. Wurster's work meant that he was directly involved in the deaths of an estimated 1.5 million people. Despite this it was decided not to charge him with any crimes and shortly after the end of the War he was promoted to become chairman of the re-established BASF. He was made an honorary professor at Heidelberg University and was given many doctorates and other awards by other universities, presumably for his work in manufacturing lethal gas. The West German Government also gave him many awards in the 1950s, also presumably for his work in making poison gas for use in gas chambers since he appears to have done nothing else of note.

Almost unbelievably, in 1959 Wurster, (who was still chairman of BASF, a former part of IG Farben) was so arrogant that he hosted a reunion banquet for the men who had worked for IG Farben, committed genocide and helped run Auschwitz during the Second World War.

The dinner was attended by Butefisch, Schneider and ter Meer among many others. The German government appears to have been perfectly happy to allow this celebratory dinner to take place and for a bunch of Nazis to toast one another. Maybe in a kindly moment during their dinner the former Nazi supporters remembered the tens of thousands of children who had lived short lives in appalling conditions and had died making them rich.

The utterly appalling Wurster retired from IG Farben in 1965 but continued to sit on the supervisory boards of a number of other German companies. According to Wikipedia, after the War, he 'became one of the leading figures in post-war Germany's industrial life.'

Surprisingly, the war criminals who had worked at IG Farben and Krupps and at other companies were allowed to keep the huge amounts of money they had made out of slavery and exploitation and genocide. Largely because of American influence, and the efforts of McCloy, there seems to have been a strong reluctance to punish businessmen, who had used the concentration camps to make money and who had provided gas and facilities for genocide, rather than actually physically turning on the gas taps themselves. The feeling at the time appears to have been that the businessmen were needed to make Germany strong again and to help create the new European federal state.

The descendants of many of the Nazi war criminals inherited the wealth their fathers had accumulated during and after the War.

The descendants of the slaves who died in the concentration camps and gas chambers inherited only sorrows.

Note 1
If you try to research these figures on the internet you will usually find that their backgrounds have been cleansed of any association with Nazis. Oddly enough, this is particularly true of individuals who are regarded by the EU as officially acceptable 'founding fathers'.

Note 2
As a curiosity, it is notable that many of the individuals listed here lived until their late 80s or 90s, though the average life expectancy of the EU's founding fathers is, of course, reduced by the fact that a number of them died suddenly in 1945 (or, in the cases of Goring and Ribbentrop, in 1946). Maybe psychopaths live longer than more sensitive individuals.

Chapter 5

Germany after World War II

In 1945, Donald MacLaren, a British spy, who had done as much as anyone to oppose IG Farben, wrote a memo on the 'De-Nazification of the German Chemical Industry'.

MacLaren believed that IG Farben had 'almost become the State itself' and that the defeat of Hitler was merely a temporary setback. His memo contains this paragraph: 'Men who built such an elaborate structure and who thought so thoroughly of every contingency in the past are not likely to disappear from the scene without leaving a group of younger men who wait for the day when our backs are turned and our interest wanes to gather again their scattered resources of money and men to engage once more in an attempt of economic domination of the world.'

MacLaren's prediction was absolutely accurate.

In modern parlance, IG Farben had become too big to be allowed to fail.

It is widely believed that all the culpable, important Nazis were either punished for their war crimes at the Nuremberg trials or that they ran away.

This is a myth.

A few of the best known Nazis were executed and a number were imprisoned but on the whole the senior Nazis who had been responsible for the most heinous crimes were found not guilty or never even charged with anything. A few (such as Krupp) whose activities were too awful to go entirely unnoticed were imprisoned but quietly released and pardoned when the attention had died down.

Around twelve thousand Germans stuffed their stolen money into travel bags, fled Europe and headed for South America where they (and their money) were welcomed and they were allowed to start new lives. The ones who took this option were either well-known and personally associated with criminal activity, and therefore very likely to be hung, or were fairly insignificant 'small fry'. The men in the first category included Josef Mengle (who fled to Paraguay and then to Brazil where he was accidentally drowned in 1979) and Adolf Eichmann (who was captured in Argentina in 1960 and hung in Israel in 1962).

The startling truth, however, is that the ambitious, powerful, patriotic and really devious Nazis all stayed in Germany because they knew that although they had lost the War, their plans would ensure that they won the peace. They also knew that their American contacts would ensure that any punishments which would be meted out would be mild and of little lasting consequence. For many of the more heinous Nazis who had their wrists slapped at the Nuremburg Tribunals the truth is that the modest punishments were little more than a passing, mild embarrassment and a minor inconvenience. Money earned during the War was not confiscated (even if it had been earned through the use of slave labour in the concentration camps) and pardons were scattered around quite freely. Numerous senior Nazis were allowed to go free because the Americans needed them to help with the creation of the new European Union.

The Nazis were delighted and probably couldn't believe their luck. But, knowing America's plans, they had prepared well for this eventuality.

In August 1944, a meeting of German industrialists was held in Strasbourg. The men at the meeting discussed how gold and art (looted from occupied countries) would be smuggled out of Germany and hidden outside Germany until it could be used to re-establish the Nazi party. At this meeting the Nazis planned how they would win the peace when they had lost the War – by taking over Europe and creating a European Union as devised by Funk et al.

According to a secret US State Department telegram dated 4th December 1945, the German Reichsbank held a huge store of gold at the Swiss National Bank. The money stolen was used by Nazis such as Hallstein to control the formation of the fledgling European Union.

As I explained earlier in this book, evidence from the BIS shows that vast sums of money which had been stored by the Nazis disappeared and could not be traced.

Surprisingly, the decision not to punish the senior Nazis was widely supported by French politicians – despite the fact that many of them had been responsible for the atrocities perpetrated in the concentration camps. So, for example, the French leader General de Gaulle insisted that Robert Schuman (now an 'official' founding father of the EU) be welcomed back into politics despite his pro-Nazi stance during the War. And in 1946, General Perrin-Pelletier, deputy French military governor, made the following press statement: 'We French take the point of view that every German was or still is a Nazi, and if you don't want to kill off all the Germans, then you have to work with these Nazis…we did not make the idiotic mistake of denazification.'

It was this sense of forgiveness, born not of compassion but of commercial and practical ambitions, which helped the Nazis build the new Germany, and the new European Union, in the style designed by Adolf Hitler and his advisers.

The Americans in Europe gave instructions that senior Nazis were not to be tried and imprisoned for several self-serving reasons – some political and some commercial.

The Americans felt that the Nazis would be needed to help rebuild Germany and to aid in the formation of the new United States of Europe. It was believed that if all the senior Nazis were punished there would be no Germans left to run the 'new' Germany and to continue with the German dream of a European Union. General Patton and other senior Americans such as Allen Dulles were concerned that without a strong Germany the powerful Soviet Union would take over Europe and provide a new, communist threat to America.

And so it was largely American influence which resulted in companies such as IG Farben going unpunished and Nazis being allowed to maintain their positions in the German power structure. General Patton in particular sabotaged the Potsdam Agreement which had called for IG Farben to be destroyed and insisted on Nazis being allowed to remain in power. He preferred the idea of Germany being run by Nazis to it being overrun by communists. Those who had made huge sums out of the concentration camps were allowed to keep their profits.

President Eisenhower had ordered that Germany should be denazified but thanks to Patton and others this did not happen and, as a result, some of the worst war criminals were put in positions where they could not only control the post war Germany but also the new pan European organisation which was being planned. Senior Nazis who had built up huge personal deposits in Swiss banks (by depositing the gold they had stolen) were allowed to take out the money and use it to build up their version of a new Germany.

In addition, rich and powerful Germans brought money back from America. They had sent vast sums to America where it stayed until after the Nuremberg trials had been completed. The money was needed to pay to fight for a German dominated Europe. Nazis agreed that their back up plan for European domination would take years to reach fruition if the War was lost but believed that their economic and political tactics would prove successful.

Since IG Farben had made a fortune out of using slave labour from concentration camps (and even had 30,000 slaves of their own at IG Auschwitz) twenty three or twenty four IG Farben executives, including Hermann Schmitz, were put on trial at Nuremberg. (There is some dispute about the precise number.) When Schmitz was detained he gave the name of the American BIS President McKittrick as a reference. Schmitz and his colleagues were regarded by prosecutors as being war criminals in the same mould as the better known Nazi leaders. They may have sat behind desks but they had, after all, been responsible for murdering and plundering millions of Jews. However, only 13 of the senior executives of IG Farben were found guilty and for those 13, the punishments were extraordinarily light. Schmitz was sentenced to just four years imprisonment (though he only served a part of this).

Astonishingly, by 1951 every single one of the IG Farben executives had been released from prison by the American high commissioner for Germany, John McCloy.

As a further 'punishment', IG Farben was broken up into four new companies (BASF, Bayer, Hoechst and Casella) and all of Farben's assets (including the profits from manufacturing the gas used in the infamous gas chambers) were transferred to the new companies – all of which were managed and run by the people who had run IG Farben.

So, the bottom line was that although IG Farben had been run by war criminals no one was really punished and things carried on much as they had done during the War. The only thing that changed was that a good deal of company notepaper had to be redesigned and freshly printed.

The new companies denied any responsibilities for the actions of IG Farben on the basis that they were new and had not existed during the War. This disgraceful self-serving legal move was accepted without a murmur of protest. Bayer, which had been a part of IG Farben, had used concentration camp victims for its experiments and for testing new drugs. The company was allowed to keep all the profits from these experiments.

The amazing truth is that the directors of IG Farben, the conglomerate which funded Hitler, ran a camp at Auschwitz and produced the gas used in the gas chambers, were allowed to play a vital part in founding the European Union in precisely the way that Walther Funk had proposed in 1940 and onwards.

By the mid-1960s, Bayer and BASF, two of the companies which were formed when IG Farben was broken up, had become ever richer and more powerful.

And there seemed to be no shame about the past. Bayer actually set up a foundation to honour a Nazi called Fritz ter Meer on his 80th birthday and started the foundation off with a donation of two million deutschmarks. (It was not until 20 years later that Bayer changed the name of the foundation.)

It did not seem to bother anyone that Herr ter Meer had overseen the building of IG Auschwitz and had handled criminal negotiations with Standard Oil. He had been found guilty of war crimes (including genocide) and sentenced to seven years imprisonment in 1948. Naturally, he did not serve the full sentence. Fritz ter Meer, one of the most evil Nazis, was released in 1950 and immediately re-joined the board of Bayer.

Within a short time of the end of the War, Hermann Abs became financial advisor in the British zone and Heinrich Dinkelbach was put in charge of all iron and steel industries in the British zone.

In 1945, Karl Blessing was arrested but he had powerful friends in two Americans: Allen Dulles and Thomas McKittrick. Like other industrialists, Blessing believed that the West would need him to help rebuild Germany and the newly planned European federation. Dulles, who knew about the work Blessing had done for Kontinental-Ol apparently didn't feel that this disqualified him for an important position, for he described Blessing as a 'prominent businessman and financial expert'. Dulles lied and said that Blessing had not been a member of the Nazi party, conveniently avoiding the fact that he had joined in 1937.

Eleanor Roosevelt was not impressed by what was going on and objected to Dulles turning a blind eye to the activities of the worst Nazis. But after her husband died her power disappeared and so Blessing was not charged with any crimes. Instead of being executed or imprisoned, Blessing returned to his job at Unilever and became one of the highest paid men in Europe. He was one of many Nazis who got rich and powerful during the War and carried their wealth and their power into the post-War years. When he died the *New York Times* newspaper published a laudatory obituary, and made no mention of concentration camps or of Blessing's 'work' with his fellow Nazis during the Second World War.

Numerous war criminals were given important posts and went completely unpunished – including many who had run the concentration camps. A report published in Germany in 1957 concluded that 77% of senior legal experts in the German Justice Ministry had previously been members of the Nazi party.

So, for example, consider the case of Heinrich Butefisch who was an employee of IG Farben and who worked at one of the Auschwitz concentration camps.

Farben had paid three reichsmarks a day for unskilled workers and one and a half reichsmarks a day for children. Workers, including children, who were too weak to work were simply murdered – since it was cheaper than keeping them alive.

Butefisch was a senior manager at the site and obviously knew exactly what was going on. As a senior manager he was responsible for thousands of murders. He was sentenced to six years imprisonment but released in 1951, under the instructions of McCloy, and almost immediately after his release, Butefisch was appointed a member of several supervisory boards – including that for Deutsche Gasolin AG. Suddenly, the horrors of Auschwitz were forgiven and forgotten. In 1964, Butefisch was awarded the Grand Cross of Merit of the Federal Republic of Germany.

Butefisch was not exceptional.

Many Nazis, particularly those who had worked for IG Farben and been responsible for the concentration camps, were very lightly punished (if at all) and were, early in the 1950s, rewarded and honoured for their 'work' in the War.

Christian Schneider was an eminent and high ranking Nazi with a powerful position at IG Farben. Schneider was tried for plunder, slavery and membership of the SS but was mysteriously acquitted on all counts. After his acquittal Schneider took important jobs at two important German companies.

The Americans who played an important part at the Nuremberg trials were more interested in helping Germany to create a federal Europe than in punishing war crimes and despite the protests of representatives from other nations, numerous Nazi war criminals went unpunished and were allowed to take important positions in German industry and public life. The Americans knew that if all the Nazis had been properly punished, Germany would have been much weakened and it would have taken much longer to create the European Union.

During the War, and particularly towards the end of it, the Nazis had taken great care to prepare for the future, for they knew that for Germany to succeed in achieving its aim of controlling Europe there would need to be many Nazis in powerful positions.

Chapter 6

The Role the Americans Played in Creating the EU

It is not widely remembered now, but during the early part of the Second World War there was much discussion in the US about whether or not America should enter the War at all. There were many powerful people who were opposed to the idea of America getting involved and there were rich and powerful people who believed that if America did become a participant then it should be on the side of the Germans rather than the British. The America First Organisation, fronted by legendary aviator Charles Lindbergh, had worked hard to persuade the US to remain neutral. Lindbergh had visited Germany and Nazis had infiltrated the organisation which was denounced by some as a Nazi front.

Early on in the War, a number of rich American businessmen felt that America should negotiate a settlement with Germany which would leave American companies in a strong position in Europe. It was thought that there would be massive financial and industrial advantages to such an agreement.

When, later, it became clear that Germany was bound to lose the War the enthusiasm for a negotiated settlement grew stronger – with American businessmen looking forward to a profitable relationship with a new German Government. And, in due course, that is exactly what happened: the Americans protected the Nazis, ensured that they were not punished, and put them back into powerful positions, first within Germany, and then within the developing European Union.

Although not common knowledge, the activities of American businessmen during the War were well documented by Charles Higham, in his book *Trading with the Enemy*. Higham explained that while British and American soldiers were fighting in Europe, Standard Oil of New Jersey supplied fuel to the Nazis, the Chase

Bank did huge amounts of business with the Nazis, Ford built trucks for German troops and that Colonel Sosthenes Behn, the head of ITT, flew to Europe to help improve Hitler's communication systems and to help improve the robot bombs being dropped on London. ITT even built the Focke-Wulfs that bombed the troops. (Amazingly, Walter Schellenberg, the Gestapo leading of counterintelligence, was a shareholder and director of ITT.) The Americans involved in these treacherous activities knew that they couldn't possibly lose. Whether Britain and America won the War, or lost it, their companies would make money.

In 1942, Donald MacLaren, a British intelligence officer, published a 70-page book entitled *Sequel to the Apocalypse: The Uncensored Story – How Your Dimes and Quarters Pay for Hitler's War*. The book, which had a foreword written by the novelist Rex Stout, described in detail the links between large German companies and American organisations. One American company, Standard Oil, was attacked for its links with IG Farben and for deliberately damaging the American war effort. Two hundred thousand copies of the book were printed but the companies named in the book bought up as many copies as possible to try to limit the damage.

According to American State Department documents, Thomas McKittrick, the pro-Nazi president of the Bank for International Settlements in Switzerland, supported by the OSS and the US State Department, was already making deals with German industrialists before the end of the War. McKittrick promised the Germans that if they cooperated then their industries would be preserved and their profits guaranteed. Since that had always been the German plan, it wasn't a difficult proposal to sell.

Two Americans, in particular, McKittrick and McCloy, were responsible for founding the European Union. McKittrick, the president of BIS, helped during the War by supporting the Nazis and by providing them with finance. The BIS helped the Nazis hide the gold they had looted. After the end of the War, it was McCloy who moved things along. It was McCloy who ensured that the imprisoned Nazis were released very quickly and that German industry, in the forms of IG Farben and Krupp Industries, was not damaged by the War. Within a remarkably short time, the men who had been responsible for the concentration camps were again running Germany. And the same men then began to manage the new pan-

European bureaucracy. (It must, of course, be remembered that McCloy did work for a law firm which represented a subsidiary of IG Farben in the United States. He was therefore connected to IG Farben.)

Both McKittrick and McCloy were clearly following orders. It seems inconceivable that McKittrick could have acted the way he did or that McCloy could have released all those German war criminals on his own initiative and without support from Washington. The key to understanding why McKittrick and McCloy acted the way they did was almost certainly Allen Dulles, the boss of the OSS (the forerunner of the CIA). Allen Dulles was resident in Switzerland throughout World War II as the local representative of the Office of Strategic Services – a secret espionage organisation which had been set up by a committee which included McCloy. Dulles lived at Herrengasse 23 in Bern throughout World War II and it is no coincidence that McKittrick and the BIS had offices just 60 miles away in Basel. After the end of the War, Allen Dulles was transferred to Berlin where John McCloy was based. One of the OSS's most important assets during the War is believed to have been Jean Monnet (the same Monnet who is now often described by the EU as one of the organisation's many 'founders').

Once the Americans became involved in the War (their decision to join the fighting was helped when the Japanese bombed Pearl Harbour) they quickly realised that they wanted to influence the look of Europe after the War had finished. More specifically, they were desperate to create a United States of Europe.

From the very beginning the EU was very much an American creation. Actually, it was more a child of the OSS (later to become the CIA) than anything else. The EU may have been conceived by the Nazis but America played the part of the midwife.

It was clear from the start that the new European Union would have to be put together around Germany. Even though Germany had just lost the Second World War it was still the strongest and richest country in Europe.

Within the space of less than 50 years, America had been involved in two costly European wars. The financial and human cost had been sickeningly high and America had no stomach for more fighting. They wanted peace and they wanted a single European nation with which they could negotiate. They also wanted a strong, united Europe to help oppose the growing power of Russia and the Soviet Union. Early on, they realised that Germany offered the best chance of a United States of Europe. It was, after all, something that Germany was desperately keen to bring to fruition, and America had enjoyed a strong relationship with Germany for many years.

Britain, the obvious choice for leadership of the new European super-state, had made it clear that it had no interest in joining any form of United States of Europe. Neither Attlee nor Churchill was interested in joining a European Union. The British had already expressed their strong distrust of any sort of European government and their determination not to join any organisation designed to unite Europe.

And there was never any question of France taking the lead when the United States of Europe was being planned. There were three reasons for this – all of them relating to the role the United States of America played in the development of the new Union.

First, and most important, France had lost two World Wars and had been badly defeated by the Germans. France had been defeated early in the Second World War, had spent several years as a German colony, had become accustomed to subservience and was clearly incapable of leading any post war organisation. The British and the Americans had been forced to rescue France from enslavement. The Americans knew it would have been absurd to expect the other countries of Europe to accept France as the leader of the group.

Second, American companies had very strong links with German countries. Before World War II there had been a sizeable part of the American population which wanted America to stay neutral – and many of those who did agree that America should be involved wanted the US to side with Germany.

Third, America had never felt close to France in the way that it felt close to Germany. There has, for many decades, been a strong and powerful German presence in America. Moreover, America had never really had much affinity with the French and didn't trust their leaders.

As far as the Americans were concerned the new EU had to be built around Germany.

Probably recognising the truth of all these factors, France was happy to be a member of a new group which would inevitably be under the control of Germany.

Today, the French enthusiasm for a United States of Europe has reached a peak under Emmanuel Macron who seems to see himself as young enough to be the first President of the new federal state.

The other most important reason for allowing Germany to control the new European super-state was that the Third Reich had already done all the preliminary spadework for a United States of Europe. Germany had conquered much of Europe and the Nazis had occupied many nations in addition to France. As we have seen, the Nazis had designed the European Union in minute detail.

The Americans felt that they could eradicate future problems by aiding and abetting the Nazi survivors in their determination to create a United States of Europe.

The Americans were keen to create a European power that could form a strong opposition to the growing might of Russia and the Soviet Union. It also seemed likely that if the constantly arguing and warring countries of Europe could be melted into a new, large, European nation there would be less aggression, less fighting and less need for America to waste money and lives helping to play the part of world policeman. And so America wanted a united Europe, preferably one controlled by Germany.

'I say no permanent solution of the German problem seems possible without an effective European union.' said John McCloy in 1950. McCloy was US High Commissioner for Germany and the man who had protected the most senior Nazis from the Nuremberg War Crimes Tribunal.

It was to aid the formation of the European Union that McCoy had arranged for many of the worst war criminals to be allowed to go free. And he had arranged for the few who were imprisoned to be released and pardoned so that they could help make Germany stronger and take part in the formation of the new European federation – later to be known as the European Union.

Germany's leaders knew (and have known all along) that they needed France to be part of their Federation. German politicians, acting according to the principles laid down by Funk and his followers, knew that they could easily create a German zone which included Austria, Luxembourg, Belgium, the Netherlands and the Eastern European countries but that if the United States of Europe were to have proper clout then France had to be included in the plan. Without French involvement the new Europe would be too obviously an extension of the Third Reich (or the beginning of a Fourth Reich). But getting France involved wasn't difficult. The French were eager to be part of the new Europe, partly because their politicians were flattered by the prospect of being significant players in the new European State and partly because, having been devastated by defeat in two wars, they were terrified of being left out of the proposals.

In the years after the formation of the European Coal and Steel Community, the Americans continued to put pressure on everyone concerned to make sure that the EU developed in the way they thought best. In 1965, an American State Department memo, sent to Robert Marjolin, the French European Commissioner (and an associate of Hallstein's), recommended that the organisation move forward to monetary union but that public discussion be avoided until 'the adoption of such proposals would become virtually inescapable'.

Ever since its formation, the European Union has been secretive about its workings and its aims and the truth has always been suppressed or manipulated.

The plan was for the new federal state of Europe to be developed quite quickly but unfortunately, nationalism and patriotism have delayed progress and Europe, particularly Southern Europe, has been irreparably damaged by the introduction of the euro. In France, Macron's dreams have been shattered by the unwillingness of the French people to accept his totalitarian EU-friendly policies.

Chapter 7

The Formation of the European Coal and Steel Community

The first step on the route to the European Union was the formation of the European Coal and Steel Community. This was done with the help of the Bank for International Settlements (BIS) and was, as with everything associated with the BIS, managed with some considerable secrecy.

It is now said that the ECSC was set up to harmonise coal and steel production in Europe and in order to encourage a sense of harmony and cooperation between Germany and its neighbours. This was, however, never the case. The ECSC was set up to ensure that the business empires of Nazis such as Krupp and Schmitz could dominate Europe.

(In 1989, as the EU prepared the launch of the euro, Jelle Zijlstra, a former Dutch Prime Minister and president of the BIS, admitted that 'The ECSC was a 'political exercise' and that the Germans 'without any doubt' regarded it as an umbrella organisation for their steel and coal cartels.)

The Post War drive for a European Union began in 1948 when 800 delegates met at The Hague to create the European Movement. The ultimate aim was simple: the creation of a federal union of European countries. It was accepted as inevitable that Germany would be the leader of the new union and that the new European federation would be created in the format designed by Walther Funk and other Nazis.

Allen Dulles, the future head of the Central Intelligence Agency, was, at the same time, setting up the American Committee for a United Europe (ACUE). The role of the ACUE was to give money to European federalists and 'use psychological warfare to campaign for a united Europe'.

The Schuman Declaration was published on 9th May 1950 and in it Robert Schuman, the French foreign minister, loosely proposed the formation of the European Coal and Steel Community. (Schuman was actually born in Luxembourg.)

Schuman's suggestion was that European countries should work together with the goal of political integration. Later, in 1958, Schuman became the first president of the forerunner of the European Parliament and is known as 'the father of Europe'. When Schuman retired, the Parliament gave him the title 'Father of Europe' and the date of 9th May was designated 'Europe Day'. In honour of Schuman's work towards a united Europe, the district housing the headquarters of several European Union institutions in Brussels is named after him.

What the European Union does not like to talk about is that Schuman supported the Nazis. After the War, the French Defence minister Andre Diethelm stated that 'this Vichy product should be immediately kicked out'. Indeed, Schuman was lucky not to have been shot as a traitor. Although Schuman, a French politician, was not a member of the Nazi party he had sworn allegiance to Marshal Petain the French Vichy leader and Nazi supporter. During the War, Schuman had himself voted to give full power to Petain and Hitler's Nazis. Schuman may not have been a member of the Nazi party (they probably wouldn't have accepted him) but he supported Hitler and was deeply involved with the Third Reich.

However, Schuman wrote to General de Gaulle to ask him to intervene. And for unknown reasons de Gaulle restored Schuman's rights as a citizen. (It can be supposed that de Gaulle was responding to pressure from the Americans who did not care how many Nazis were running Europe as long as there was a united Europe.)

The European Coal and Steel Community (ECSC), the harmless sounding supranational institution which became the European Union, was officially founded in 1951. The German steel and coal industrialists who had supported Schlotterer's original plan (qv) were behind this organisation. It was immediately suggested that the ECSC should develop into a military alliance.

The same industrialists who had put Hitler in power (the ones working at IG Farben, Thyssen and Krupp) were the men who created the European Coal and Steel Community.

One of the founding members of the ECSC was Walter Hallstein, the Nazi army officer and propagandist who first came to prominence after speaking at a Nazi conference in 1939. Hallstein used the same constructions and phraseology which had been devised for bringing occupied countries into line and which he had used in Hitler's Germany. Hallstein would later become the first President of the EU Commission.

The third well-known member of the ECSC was Konrad Adenauer.

Adenauer repeatedly claimed that he had not been a Nazi but admitted that he had violated Prussian laws in order to allow Nazi events in public buildings and Nazi flags to be flown from city flagpoles. In 1932, he had publicly declared that the Nazis should join the Reich government in a leading role. Technically, Adenauer was not a member of the Nazi party but he knowingly appointed many Nazis to his government when he was German chancellor – and defended them when questioned.

The other six members of the ECSC were fairly irrelevant. One, Dirk Sticker, had been a director of the Heineken beer company during the War. Another, Count Carlo Sforza – was a member of the Italian Government during the War. The Italians were, of course, allies of Nazi Germany

When the ECSC was founded an attempt was made to give the organisation an air of democracy by providing a Common Assembly. This was a 'consultative assembly' of parliamentarians drawn from the parliaments of member states. The Common Assembly had no legislative powers. Over the years the Common Assembly has morphed into the much grander and infinitely more expensive European Parliament. The European Parliament still has no legislative powers. It can discuss decisions made by the European Commission (the executive branch of the European Union, staffed entirely by eurocrats who have been appointed or hired rather than elected) but it cannot overrule them and is not a proper legislature. There has never been any suggestion that the European Union could ever become a democratic institution.

Chapter 8

Britain Says No to the European Coal and Steel Community (and the EU)

In 1950, when the first plans were put forward for a pan European trade organisation, the British Government made it clear that Britain would not be interested in joining.

Clement Attlee, Britain's Prime Minister at the time, was one of the first to recognise the problems and disadvantages associated with the planned European unity. He was, in particular, concerned about the lack of democratic control and the lack of sovereignty that membership of any sort of union would require.

When responding to the Schuman plan for the European Coal and Steel Community (the initial version of the EU) he said: 'It (is) impossible for Britain to accept the principle that the economic forces of this country should be handed over to an authority that is utterly undemocratic and is responsible to nobody.'

It has frequently been claimed by EU officials and supporters that Sir Winston Churchill was an enthusiastic supporter of the EU and would have voted Remain – to stay in the European Union.

This is a lie and so far removed from the truth as to be laughable.

The fact was that Churchill knew that the EU was Hitler's dream and he, like Attlee, was completely opposed to the idea of Britain joining any European organisation which threatened Britain's independence in any way.

'Britain could not be an ordinary member of a federal union limited to Europe in any period which can be…foreseen.' – Winston Churchill.

'If you ask me to choose between Europe and the open sea, I choose the open sea.' – Winston Churchill.

'We are with Europe but not of it. We are linked, but not compromised. We are interested and associated but not absorbed...for we dwell among our own people.' – Winston Churchill.

And so, with its leading politicians (other than Oswald Moseley) completely opposed to the idea, Britain took no part in the formation of the ECSC. The new organisation would be totally dominated by Germany. And that meant that it would, inevitably, be designed and built according to the plans laid down by the Nazis. Moreover, it would be largely staffed and controlled by Nazis and Nazi supporters.

The organisation was formed to strengthen Germany and to exploit economically weak countries (such as Greece and those in Eastern Europe). The institution was always designed to be undemocratic and accountable to the German elite rather than the people of Europe.

This is as true of today's European Union as it was of the ECSC. It should be no surprise that other countries which are members of the European Union frequently complain that the organisation is run by and for Germany.

That was always the plan.

Sadly, Attlee's refusal and Churchill's complete lack of interest were not to thwart the European Union for long.

The pressure for Britain to join the EU came from the United States of America.

And it was always known that the plan was for the EU to become a super-state: the United States of Europe.

In 1961, American President John Kennedy told British Prime Minister, Harold Macmillan that the White House would only support Britain's application to join the Common Market (as the EU was then generally known) if Britain accepted that the true goal of the Common Market was political integration – Hitler's famous United States of Europe.

And in1966, American President Lyndon Johnson encouraged Britain's membership of what was now called the European Economic Community. In London, Foreign Office civil servants decided that the 'special relationship' with the USA would be enhanced if Britain joined. Britain's membership of the EEC was dealt with in great secrecy.

In January 1973, Britain finally joined the Common Market (along with Denmark and the Republic of Ireland). The treaty which took Britain into the Market was signed by Edward Heath – a self-confessed liar and, without a doubt, a traitor. It is widely believed that Heath did not have the legal and constitutional power to sign the document and that it was, therefore, illegal.

In 1975, under a new Labour Government, the Prime Minister, Harold Wilson, organised a Referendum on whether Britain should stay in the Common Market. The campaign to stay in was heavily subsidised by the Government and the Common Market and almost all the British press campaigned for voters to maintain membership.

During that Referendum campaign, Edward Heath said: 'There is no question of any erosion of essential national sovereignty.'

The result of the referendum was a victory for those wanting Britain to retain its membership of the Common Market. (There was, of course, no question of the referendum being rerun to give those wanting to leave a second chance at victory.)

Heath knew that he was lying when he said that there would be no loss of sovereignty.

The Lord Chancellor had written to Heath saying: 'I must emphasise that in my view the surrenders of sovereignty involved are serious ones…these objections ought to be brought into the open.'

An internal Foreign Office memorandum argued that the British people would not notice what had happened until the end of the 20th century, by which time it would be far too late to do anything about it.

In 1998, Heath was asked if he had known that joining the Common market would lead to a federal Europe. 'Of course I bloody did,' he replied.

Heath received a tax free 'prize' of approximately £35,000 for knowingly and fraudulently selling his country to the German dominated Common Market.

Within a few years, the Common Market had gradually been transformed into the European Union.

Chapter 9

How and Why the Media (Particularly the BBC) Protects the EU

Large media organisations traditionally try to reflect the interests, enthusiasms, beliefs and political hopes of their readers (the electors). However, the way that the media in Britain deals with the European Union has been the solitary exception to this rule.

Before the Referendum was held, the media in Britain was almost entirely supportive of the European Union.

And even after the Referendum, when the British people surprised and startled the Establishment by voting convincingly to leave the EU, the establishment media remained largely supportive of the EU and overtly, and sometimes cruelly, critical of those who had voted to leave the EU.

It isn't difficult to explain the media's enthusiasm for the European Union – though different branches of the media seem to have their own reasons for supporting an organisation which was founded by Nazis and which regards democracy as an unnecessary luxury.

The BBC has for years been consistently pro-EU and before the Referendum it was clear that the Corporation regarded the very idea of leaving the EU as sacrilegious. Even though the Corporation is funded by a compulsory licence fee taken from a largely unwilling and often rather resentful electorate, the BBC has deliberately favoured the minority point of view – the one espoused by Remainers.

In no area of politics has the BBC been so utterly devoted to one point of view as it has in the area of European integration.

In the months after the nation decided it no longer wanted to be ruled by a bunch of unelected bureaucrats living and working in Belgium, the BBC did everything it could to demonise Brexit and

Brexiteers. On the relatively rare occasions when Brexit supporters were allowed into a studio, they were invariably labelled 'right wing' and treated as though they were in some way criminal. On the other hand, when Remainers were interviewed they were treated with great respect and introduced as though they were independent commentators.

It became quite well known that when the BBC arranged a programme with an audience then the audience would be packed with Remainers.

Every piece of bad news was (sometimes laughably) blamed on Brexit and every piece of good news was accompanied by the phrase 'despite Brexit'.

Studies of the BBC have shown an overwhelming bias against Brexit.

Here are some facts that all licence fee payers should know:

The BBC charter demands that the BBC is impartial and reflects all strands of public opinion. In return for this impartiality, the BBC is entitled to an annual licence fee (currently around £150).

But the BBC is NOT impartial. To give but one example, between 2005 and 2015, the Today programme welcomed 4,275 guests to discuss the EU. Just 132 of them were Brexiteers.

This bias has been going on for years. Way back in 2004, a study conducted by the Centre for Policy Studies revealed that the BBC gave twice as much coverage to pro-EU speakers as to eurosceptics.

Since it has been established that the EU was created by Nazis to further the interests of Germany, it seems clear that the BBC has for years been supporting Nazi policies.

I suspect that not a few citizens will be appalled to find that they are being forced to give money to a Corporation which many might well regard as a neo-Nazi organisation which has been bought by the EU. The BBC is a corrupt and traitorous organisation which has betrayed Britain and the British. I believe the BBC is in breach of its own Charter and no longer entitled to the annual licence fee. Far from being expected to continue paying money to the BBC, citizens of Britain are entitled to receive refunds for the money they have handed over in the past.

The worst thing about the BBC's affection for and loyalty to the European Union is that it was not inspired solely by a misplaced belief within the BBC that they know best.

The truth is simpler: the BBC has been bought by the European Union. In one recent five year period, the BBC accepted 258 million euros from the EU. Over the recent years the BBC has accepted huge quantities of EU money.

So it is no surprise that the BBC is biased in favour of the European Union.

The BBC even allows its anti-Brexit feeling to intrude on programmes which have nothing to do with news or politics. The 2018 edition of the Last Night of the Proms was ruined for many by the fact that television screens seemed to show interminable waving of EU flags. The 2019 BAFTA awards were edited and not shown as live but the BBC still managed to leave in anti-Brexit comments which for many viewers seemed jarring and utterly inappropriate.

The BBC seems to repay the financial support it receives from the EU (which it receives in addition to the licence fee payments British citizens are forced to pay) by opposing Brexit, by defending unpopular EU policies (such as those on immigration), by insisting that all measurements referred to in its programmes are in EU friendly metric units rather than proper British imperial measurements and by taking every opportunity to disparage England and the English.

It is, I think, now widely recognised that BBC journalists (like many of their colleagues working for other branches of the media) seem to have lost the ability to differentiate between 'news' and 'comment'.

Civitas, an independent think tank, has commented that 'the BBC pays lip service to impartiality but acts more like a political party with a policy manifesto.'

And this partisan approach to the news is not confined to Brexit and the European Union.

When Donald Trump was elected President of the United States of America, the BBC reported the event with sneery comments on his opinions, his political views and his personality. And when the BBC reported his policies on immigration, they did so as though they were eccentric and extreme, although every poll showed that a majority of Americans and a majority of Europeans agreed with Trump's policies. Whenever Trump is mentioned the disdain is almost palpable.

However, whenever the EU supporting Obama is mentioned, the BBC drools with affection – never mentioning the former President's crafty deceits and the broken promises.

Moreover, the BBC appears to have a deep contempt for populism; a movement which has become global and which worries the political establishment so much that they dismiss it in the same sort of tone which you might expect them to use for fascism or communism. Here again, the BBC's attitude is irrational for populism is defined as a movement that champions 'the common person' in preference to the interests of the establishment. Populism invariably combines people on both the left and the right and is invariably hostile to large banks, large multinational corporations and extremists of all kinds. You might think that an organisation which is paid for by the populace at large might have at least a little sympathy with their interests, needs and anxieties. But, no, the BBC has firmly allied itself with the ruling classes and the Europhilic establishment and has no time for licence fee payers who are concerned about mass immigration, overcrowding, relentless globalisation and absurdly ill-based 'green' policies which result in new laws which have pushed up energy prices so dramatically that millions of hard working people have to choose between eating and keeping warm.

The inevitable result is that the people who pay the BBC licence fee (and enable it to pay out multimillion pound salaries to presenters) no longer have much time for the BBC.

In his excellent and comprehensive book *BBC: Brainwashing Britain*, David Sedgwick reports that a survey of 39,341 people showed that 85% of Britons no longer trust BBC News to give unbiased political coverage. Sedgwick claims that the BBC is now guilty of brainwashing the people of Britain; using tricks and subterfuges to deceive and promote its own position. There is little doubt that the discerning public (the people who pay the licence fee and keep the BBC well fed and fat) have had quite enough of the Corporation and would happily see it die.

Celebrities commonly speak out in support of the BBC and endorse its line on most things (especially Brexit) but it is difficult not to suspect that this is because they fear that if they don't then they will be ostracised and will no longer be offered well paid acting or presenting jobs. The BBC infuriates its paymasters (the licence fee payers) by allowing one of its best paid presenters to use his status to attack Brexit.

Most people now recognise that the BBC represents a minority viewpoint and gives absurd amounts of airtime and respect to the high priests and priestesses of political correctness. (This may be because, as one senior BBC figure has pointed out, the BBC has 'an abnormally large number of young people, ethnic minorities and gay people' on its staff. The BBC 'has a liberal bias' admitted the presenter.)

The BBC is not a broadcaster it is a narrowcaster; a propaganda unit for the elite. It is hardly surprising that Sedgwick reports that nearly ten million people cancelled their TV licences between 2007 and 2017. Thanks to the EU's policies, espoused by the BBC, the UK's population has soared but the number of licence fee holders has plummeted.

Moreover, the viewing figures for many BBC shows have sunk dramatically and in the last couple of decades the viewing figures for the BBC's news programmes have shown a decline that would have startled any broadcaster which did not have the State's authority to collect money from millions of unwilling citizens. The position is now so bad that if the BBC loses its licence fee then it will die because it will be unable to find enough viewers prepared to subscribe to its services. If the BBC retains its anachronistic right to demand licence fees then the annual charge must rocket to counterbalance the fall in the number of people prepared to pay the fee.

The simple truth is that today's BBC is Biased, Bought and Corrupt and it isn't difficult to find the evidence showing this.

BBC employees show little or no loyalty to their country or to the long suffering licence fee payers who, as employers, deserve considerably more respect than they receive.

Joseph Goebbels, the Minister of Propaganda in the Third Reich, would have been proud of the BBC.

Of course, the BBC is not the only media organisation which supports the European Union and takes every opportunity to attack Brexit and Brexiteers.

The *Financial Times* has always been enthusiastic about the EU and in a way this doesn't seem to me to be particularly surprising. The EU was designed and built to promote the interests of large businesses and to suppress small businesses which might in some way prove threatening to the profitability of multinationals. The only real purpose of the EU is to ensure that a limited number of large companies (particularly German ones) can successfully control trade. It is important also to remember that the Americans helped create the European Union and that one of the intentions was to enable large American companies to profit from the EU's unique brand of fascism.

It would be more surprising if the *Financial Times* had not supported the European Union.

Like the BBC, the *Financial Times* takes every opportunity to warn about the dangers of Brexit and to attack those who support national independence, personal freedom and the basic principles of democracy. After all, those are not qualities which are likely to prove profitable for financial institutions such as Goldman Sachs.

There have been some media surprises.

Those who voted to leave the EU were doubtless startled when the *Daily Mail* changed its policy regarding the European Union in 2018.

When a new pro-EU editor called Geordie Grieg was appointed, the *Daily Mail* started to sympathise with Remainers who wanted the country to stay in the EU. The previous editor of the *Daily Mail*, Paul Dacre, had been strongly opposed to the European Union. (It must be remembered, however, that the *Daily Mail* gave extraordinary editorial support to Gordon Brown, the Prime Minister who signed the Lisbon Treaty in 2007. The Lisbon Treaty was, of course, the bullet which put freedom and democracy into intensive care.).

The switch in policy of the *Daily Mail* surprised many but there is a strong historical precedent. The *Daily Mail* has 'history'.

In the 1930s, a previous Viscount Rothermere was a strong supporter of Nazi Germany and a keen supporter of fascism. In 1934, the *Daily Mail* published an article by Rothermere (the paper's proprietor) entitled 'Hurrah for the Blackshirts'. The article praised Oswald Moseley.

Rothermere met Adolf Hitler many times and when Germany began invading other parts of Europe (such as Czechoslovakia), he wrote to the Fuhrer with support. He also said he hoped that 'Adolf the Great' would become a popular figure in Britain. Moreover,

Rothermere actually paid a huge annual retainer to a German spy; apparently hoping that she would bring him closer to Hitler.

So, it is perhaps not as surprising as it might appear to be that the latest edition of Lord Rothermere should now produce a newspaper which supports Hitler's greatest legacy – the European Union.

Even the internet now appears to take a pro EU line.

Many of the Wikipedia sites which deal with the former Nazis who played a vital role in the formation of the European Union have been cleansed of any uncomfortable references. It is now a well-known 'fact' that almost all the Nazis who did terrible things in World War II only did them because they were forced to do so by men with guns and bayonets. Even the men with the guns and the bayonets only did what they did because they were afraid for their lives. If you look at the reports of the Nuremberg trials it appears that Hitler and a couple of close allies were the only people willingly fighting World War II. All the other members of the Nazi party joined up because they were afraid. All the soldiers and prison camp guards who were responsible for unspeakable atrocities did what they did because they had no choice.

(When it was revealed that the father of Juncker, the President of the European Commission, had been a Nazi soldier the usual excuse was dragged out. We were told that he only became a Nazi because he had no choice. Juncker found it more difficult to explain away his father-in-law who had been a Nazi propaganda chief in charge of enforcing a law which stripped Jews of their rights.)

The European Union's propaganda machine must be admired for its thoroughness in cleansing much of the internet of material which might otherwise be embarrassing. However, the EU has not been able to get rid of the books which tell the history of World War II and those who might like to read more accurate analyses and biographies than appear on Wikipedia would be well advised to take a look at the very short bibliography at the back of this book.

However, there is no doubt that the censorship continues, and will continue.

Not surprisingly, the German press has been particularly vitriolic in its attacks on those in Britain who are desperate to leave the EU and regain their sovereignty. And the German media has been eagerly collecting British celebrities to support the European Union and to criticise their countrymen for their affection for sovereignty, freedom and democracy. Not a few have made treasonous statements criticising their own country and praising the enemy. When listening to the hysterical, treacherous voices of British celebrities it has been difficult to suppress the thought of William Joyce, Lord Haw Haw, broadcasting during World War Two.

'The British who voted to leave are stupid,' said one eminent German. ('But at least we didn't vote for Hitler and lose two World Wars' was one pithy and entirely reasonable response.)

Even social media seems to have chosen to side with the European Union.

Jack King, the author of the book *Indisputable Evidence Proving the EU was Created by Nazis* reports that when he decided to open a twitter campaign to initiate a conversation about the history of the EU, he found himself banned with his very first attempted tweet. When he tried to publish a tweet explaining that the EU was created by Nazis (an entirely accurate allegation), he received notification that he had been banned to protect the Twitter community.

Appendix 1: A Dozen Ways the EU Has Wrecked Life in Britain

Over the years we've given billions in membership fees to the EU. In return they have damaged Britain in scores of ways. Here are a few:

The EU has wrecked the NHS. The EU's Working Time Directive means that GPs and hospital doctors are not allowed to work more than 40 hours a week. The NHS spends millions on policing doctors' working hours to make sure that EU laws are not broken. It is entirely due to the EU's laws that patients can no longer get hold of a GP at nights or at the weekend. The licensing scheme introduced for doctors has pushed thousands of doctors into early retirement and the insistence that large numbers of women doctors be trained has resulted in a reduced medical workforce. (Many female doctors choose to work part time.) As a fascist organisation (designed to satisfy the requirements of large companies) the EU believes that 'big is beautiful' and it is because of the EU that local hospitals have been closed leaving millions of patients many miles from the nearest hospital. The massive increase in population resulting from enforced immigration has put pressure on the NHS at a time when the service was being reduced. The result of the EU interference is that medical care in the UK is now considerably worse than it was half a century ago. Moreover, things will continue to get worse. It is EU policy to close down the NHS which does not fit into the EU's plans for European health care.

Energy costs have soared because of the EU's absurd regulations. The bills have gone up because pseudoscientists have convinced eurocrats that climate change is a reality. As a result of the EU's daft policies electricity supplies will soon run out.

The cost of food has rocketed because of the Common Agriculture Policy – designed to enrich lazy and inefficient French farmers.

Recycling is an EU nonsense. It is the EU's fault that we no longer have weekly bin collections. Recycling materials are taken overseas to be dumped, buried or burnt. And councils are fined by the EU if they don't follow the mad rules dreamt up by hysterical eurocrats.

Interest rates are kept at absurdly low rates to protect European bankers. The result is that savers and pensioners have suffered and house prices have soared – making property too expensive for young folk.

Roads are too busy and full of potholes because of overcrowding (England is the most crowded country in Europe).

Schoolchildren are growing up unable to read or write because many immigrants cannot speak English and educational standards have fallen.

Small businesses are failing because of EU employment laws and other legislation – many of which have been introduced on behalf of multinational corporations who have used vast armies of lobbyists to influence EU legislation. (Lobbying is just another word for corruption. Lobbyists are hired by rich companies to influence politicians. There are more lobbyists than politicians, journalists or EU employees working in Brussels.)

The EU gave us VAT. The value added tax system was introduced throughout Europe and it, like much EU legislation, has had its greatest impact on the poor – pushing millions into poverty.

Mass immigration of citizens from poorer EU countries has resulted in the lowering of wages and living standards for millions of Britons. Zero hours contracts were introduced as a result of EU legislation. The overcrowding has put unbearable pressure on all aspects of Britain's infrastructure. The idea of allowing immigrants to flood into countries such as the UK is to break up the identity of individual countries. Mass immigration is sold as an essential way of dealing with the problems said to be associated with an ageing population but for the EU it has useful side effects too – it helps to destroy local culture and to demoralise the population.

EU legislation has destroyed pensions for those who do not work for the Government or the Bank of England.

EU laws are responsible for our loss of privacy and freedom.

The EU's ostensibly liberal and Green policies have pushed millions of Europeans into poverty. Economic policies designed to enrich Germany have resulted in horrendous levels of unemployment in Italy, Greece and other southern European countries. Food laws have enriched farmers (especially in France) but have pushed up the price of food. Energy policies designed to satisfy wealthy German Greens have pushed up the cost of energy and fuel throughout Europe and have made life miserable for millions who now have to choose between eating and heating. People living in rural communities have been particularly badly damaged by the EU's policies. (The recent protests in France were triggered largely by rural citizens complaining that Macron's pro-EU policies had pushed up the cost of diesel and made their lives impossible.) New laws inspired by lobbyists and designed to enrich multinational corporations have killed entrepreneurship in Europe.

It is no exaggeration to say that the dafter a piece of legislation appears to be, and the more harm it does, the more certain it is that the legislation originated in Brussels. The EU is replete with hidden agendas. Indefensible recycling regulations and absurd climate change laws have been introduced to disguise the reality of the fact that the world's oil supplies are shrinking. Oil needs to be preserved for official purposes and the public must be weaned off their usual energy supplies and forced to accept new, more expensive alternatives immediately.

Perhaps the most absurd example of the way Germany now controls Europe is the fact that parts for British army tanks are now made in Germany. The tank was invented by Britain during the First World War but today it is Germany which controls tank production.

Appendix 2: How EU Employees are forced to Remain Loyal

Employees of the EU are extraordinary well paid and in addition to huge tax free salaries, incredibly short working hours, long holidays and perks that would astonish employees anywhere else, the EU's employees are also entitled to massive pensions (which are paid for by Europe's taxpayers).

There is, however, one oddity.

Former employees of the EU must remain completely loyal to the EU if they wish to continue to receive their pension. They must be loyal and they must never offer any criticism of the organisation. (The views of former EU employees should be considered with this in mind.)

Can you imagine employees of any other organisation being prepared to put up with such a rule?

The unions would, rightly, create an uproar if, for example, former employees of the National Health Service might lose their pensions if they dared to criticise the organisation.

But this is how the EU operates.

Inconvenient truths must always be suppressed.

The EU, like the Nazis, believes in using fear, deceit, misdirection and bullying to defend itself.

Appendix 3: Basic Bibliography

Below I have listed a few of the many books used as reference sources in preparing this book. In addition to these (and many other books) I referred to hundreds of articles, documents and websites.

One warning: it is necessary to take great care when using websites. Many websites have been prepared to put forward a particular point of view and a number which deal with the European Union and with individual Nazis appear to have been 'cleansed' to protect the EU. Much of the information in this book can be found on the internet by an assiduous researcher but it has to be said that some 'cleansing' has been done of inconvenient personal histories. Many of those who are now known to have found the EU appear to have exemplary wartime records. Wikipedia entries for some former Nazis appeared to have been 'cleansed'. Is it possible that the EU has been tidying up its own history?

For those who want to know more about the European Union, I heartily recommend *OFPIS* by Vernon Coleman (known in some circles as the 'anti-Funk') and *The EU: The Truth about the Fourth Reich* by Daniel J. Beddowes and Flavio Cipollini, whose campaigning has exposed many of the EU's deceits.

Lest it be thought that only British and American authors have drawn attention to the history of the EU, I should point out that German historians have, on a number of occasions published documents detailing the background to the European Union.

In 1972, Gerhardt Haas and Wolfgang Schumann published a collection of documents entitled *The Anatomy of Aggression: New documents concerning the military goals of German imperialism during the Second World War*. The documents they collected showed how the Nazi leadership were planning the economic integration of Europe. These were not just a few dreams put together by oddball Nazis. The plans were devised by the Reich Ministry of Economics, the Reich Industrial Group and the Reich Ministry of Foreign Affairs.

In 1985, Michael Zalewski published *Plans for a Continental European Union:1939-1945* in which he published details of the integration planned by the German leadership during the Second World War.

In 1987, another collection of German documents detailing the way the Third Reich planned European integration was prepared by Hans Werner Neulen and called *Europe and the Third Reich*. Once again the impact of the publication was reduced by the efficiency of the propaganda machine of the European Union.

These publications all show that phrases such as 'European Union' and 'European Economic Community' were all described as being official elements of state policy in documents published by Adolf Hitler's Third Reich.

Naturally, the information contained in these publications has been effectively drowned by misinformation published and disseminated by and on behalf of the European Union.

Atkinson R and McWhirter N – *Treason at Maastricht: Destruction of the Nation State*

Banks, Arron – *The Bad Boys of Brexit*

Beddowes, D & Cippolini – *The EU: The Truth About the Fourth Reich: How Adolf Hitler Won the Second World War*

Bernstein, Larry – *Fog Facts*

Bower, Tom – *Blind Eye to Murder: Britain, America and the Purging of Nazi Germany – a Pledge Betrayed*

Coleman, Vernon – *England Our England*

Coleman, Vernon – *The OFPIS File*

Freemantle, Brian – *The Octopus (Europe in the Grip Of Organised Crime)*

Goodwin M & Milazzo C – *UKIP Inside the Campaign to Redraw the Map of British Politics*

Hallstein, Walter – *Europe in the Making*

Hartrich, Edwin – *The Fourth and Richest Reich*

Haas G & Schumann W – *The Anatomy of Aggression: New documents concerning the military goals of German imperialism during the Second World War. (1972)*

Higham, Charles – *Trading with the Enemy – An Expose of the Nazi-American Money Plot 1933-1949*

King, Jack – *Indisputable Evidence Proving the EU was Created by Nazis*

Laughland, John – *The Tainted Source*

Lebor, Adam – *Tower of Basel (The Shadowy History of the Secret Bank that Runs the World)*

Neulen, Hans Werner – *Europe and the Third Reich (1987)*

Pol, Heinz – *The Hidden Enemy (The German Threat to Post War Peace)*

Salter, Sir Arthur – *The United States of Europe*

Zalewski, Michael – *Plans for a Continental European Union: 1939-1945 (1985)*

Appendix 4: We Must Destroy the EU

The European Union is an evil organisation. It was created by evil men for evil purposes.

The only way to defeat the European Union, and to protect our freedom and democracy, is to destroy it completely.

And the only way to do this is to tell the truth about how, why and when it was designed and created.

Please tell everyone you know the facts about the formation of the European Union.

Author's Note
If you have found this book illuminating, I would be enormously grateful if you would write a short, favourable review on Amazon, Goodreads and other sites.